Your Towns and Cities in the Great War

# Durham City in the Great War

Your Towns and Cities in the Great War

# Durham City in the Great War

Stephen Wynn

Pen & Sword
**MILITARY**

First published in Great Britain in 2017 by
PEN & SWORD MILITARY
*an imprint of*
Pen and Sword Books Ltd
47 Church Street
Barnsley
South Yorkshire S70 2AS

Copyright © Stephen Wynn, 2017

ISBN 978 1 78303 032 3

The right of Stephen Wynn to be identified as the author of this work has been asserted by him in accordance with the Copyright, Designs and Patents Act 1988.

A CIP record for this book is available from the British Library

All rights reserved. No part of this book may be reproduced or transmitted in any form or by any means, electronic or mechanical including photocopying, recording or by any information storage and retrieval system, without permission from the Publisher in writing.

Printed and bound in England
by CPI Group (UK) Ltd, Croydon, CR0 4YY

Typeset in Times New Roman by Chic Graphics

*Pen & Sword Books Ltd incorporates the imprints of*
Pen & Sword Archaeology, Atlas, Aviation, Battleground, Discovery, Family History, History, Maritime, Military, Naval, Politics, Railways, Select, Social History, Transport, True Crime, Claymore Press, Frontline Books, Leo Cooper, Praetorian Press, Remember When, Seaforth Publishing and Wharncliffe.

*For a complete list of Pen and Sword titles please contact*
Pen and Sword Books Limited
47 Church Street, Barnsley, South Yorkshire, S70 2AS, England
E-mail: enquiries@pen-and-sword.co.uk
Website: www.pen-and-sword.co.uk

# Contents

|   | Introduction: A Brief History of Durham and the Outbreak of War, 1914 | 6 |
|---|---|---|
|   | Sources | 8 |
| 1 | 1914: Starting Out | 9 |
| 2 | 1915: Deepening Conflict | 33 |
| 3 | 1916: The Realization | 57 |
| 4 | 1917: Seeing It Through | 75 |
| 5 | 1918: The Final Push | 93 |
| 6 | Voluntary Aid Detachments | 107 |
| 7 | The Aftermath | 119 |
| 8 | First World War Memorials in Durham | 125 |
|   | Index | 143 |

# Introduction:

# A Brief History of Durham and the Outbreak of War, 1914

The history of Durham City, which sits proudly upon the River Weir, can be traced as far back as AD 995, when the world truly was a different place. But its origins really began 200 years before that, at around the time that the Christian faith started spreading across the country. One of those who was encouraging others to follow the teachings of Jesus Christ, was Cuthbert, who after having decided on becoming a monk at a relatively young age, became the Bishop of Lindisfarne. He eventually decided on pursuing the life of a hermit and set up home on the small and remote island of Inner Farne.

On his death in AD 687, his body was taken to Lindisfarne and buried. A few years later, so the story goes, monks decided to inspect his body and, on opening his coffin, found that his body had not decayed. This discovery was determined to be a miracle and Cuthbert was made a saint. Whether it was a miracle or not is open to conjecture, but either way, it made the monks and their monastery at Lindisfarne extremely wealthy as Cuthbert's story and the island began attracting literarily boatloads of pilgrims. But because of the continued Viking raids during throughout the ninth century, the monks of Lindisfarne decided to vacate the island and take St Cuthbert's coffin with them. So it was that in the year AD 995 it eventually ended up in the City of Durham.

The city has seen many changes over the years. In 1006, with the help of the high peninsula that the city was built upon, the inhabitants defeated an invading Scottish horde who wanted the wealth that the new city had amassed. Some visitors were welcomed, the people who came to the city as pilgrims, to worship at the cathedral. Others included King Canute and William the Conqueror, the latter most definitely not a pilgrim.

The city continued to prosper over the years and through the ages it went from strength to strength, due in no small part to the influence and power of the Bishops of Durham. Armies have been raised, the city has held its own Parliament, it has minted its own coins and administered its own laws, to name but a few of its advantages. During the reign of King Henry VIII, the Bishop's powers were somewhat reduced, and in 1538, as if to prove a point of who really did hold power, the King ordered the destruction of the sacred shrine of Saint Cuthbert.

During the English Civil War, which took place between 1640 and 1660, the city remained loyal to King Charles I. The cathedral was closed in 1650 as part of the aftermath of the abolition of the Church of England and the closure of numerous religious buildings.

In the country's first ever national census, carried out in 1801, Durham was recorded as having a population of 7,100, showing how it was going from strength to strength, with its main industries being those of weaving and coal. In 1825 the world's first-ever passenger railway line came into being in the city. By 1832 it had its first university. The castle, which had previously been the home to the Bishop of Durham, became the University College of Durham after the incumbent bishop, William Van Mildert, moved into Auckland Castle. Therefore Durham Castle has been in continuous use for the past 900 years and remains the only castle in the United Kingdom that never fell to an attacker.

Throughout its history Durham had seen plenty of fighting and death, so war was certainly nothing new to its people. But the First World War would be a war like no other before it. A clash of the ages as the era of cavalry being top dog finally came to an end as they were replaced with mechanized vehicles, heavy artillery, machine guns, flamethrowers, chemical weapons and aircraft. The killing that was to come over the next four years would be carried out on an almost industrial scale, the like of which had never been seen before.

The alliances that were in place between so many countries, as nations rushed to protect themselves from attack, in an ever-changing European landscape, in increasingly volatile times, always had the potential for catastrophe.

Napoleon had tried to totally dominate Europe a hundred years earlier, and had nearly succeeded, mainly due to the fact that nations did not have treaties binding them together in times of danger. Lessons were learnt and nations began aligning themselves with friendly nations for protection, just in case they were threatened by an aggressor. Nobody seemed to realize the potential consequences of what these alliances might bring with them, or if they did, they simply appear to have crossed their fingers and hoped for the best. Maybe the hope was that by being in place these alliances would be a sufficient deterrent to prevent war altogether, similar to today's nuclear deterrent.

*  *  *

# Sources

www.cwgc.co.uk
www.ancestry.co.uk
www.britishnewspaperarchive.co.uk
Wikipedia
www.warpoets.org.uk
www.durhamrecordoffice.org.uk
www.redcross.org.uk
www.scarletfinders.com
www.naval-history.net

CHAPTER 1

# 1914
# Starting Out

By 11 pm on 4 August 1914, Great Britain would be at war with Germany. Although the time given for the ultimatum for Germany to be out of Belgium had not been adhered to, it would have been more of a shock if war had not begun than if it had. The government in Berlin had decided that their best course of action was to say nothing in return.

But preparations were already in hand throughout the United Kingdom. At just after four o'clock in the morning on Tuesday, 4 August 1914 a train arrived at Durham Railway Station in North Road. On board were soldiers from the 8th Battalion, Durham Light Infantry, a Territorial unit which had just returned from their annual camp at Conway in North Wales. On their arrival they marched through the

*An early war recruitment poster.*

streets of Durham before coming to a halt in the market square where some of the battalion set up an improvised camp which included a field kitchen, whilst the remainder carried on to the Drill Hall at nearby Gilesgate.

A second train arrived at North Road railway station an hour later at, which saw the arrival of even more members of the 8th Battalion,

*A family soon to be separated by the war.*

*Durham Light Infantry Band – officers in the front row.*

who then marched off to join their colleagues, led by the regimental band. During the course of the day the men drew much attention from inquisitive members of the public, who were intrigued to see them cooking and singing in the town square.

To add to the excitement and furore of the City's market square having been taken over by men in khaki, was the sight and sound of the Royal Field Artillery and their large artillery pieces trundling through the streets later in the day, on their way to be put in place as part of the north-east coastal defence system.

* * *

On Tuesday, 11 August 1914, with the war entering its second week, a public meeting took place at Durham Town Hall. It had been called for the purpose of enabling men, who for a variety of reasons were unable to enlist in the armed forces, to do their bit on the home front should the need occur.

For some it was business reasons, whilst for others it was because of family matters, which meant that they just couldn't rush off to war, even if they had wanted to, a business that needed somebody to physically be there to run it on a daily basis, or ailing parents who would have nobody to look after them, their only option then to become inmates at the local workhouse. The men who couldn't go were more than happy to serve in a locally-based civilian corps, whilst still going about their daily business.

The Mayor of Durham, Councillor Charles Caldcleugh, who presided over the meeting, opened proceedings by saying that the war which the country now found itself embroiled in, was one which had been forced upon them by Germany and her emperor. He continued the patriotic rhetoric by declaring that Britain needed to sweep the German fleet from the seas, words which were met with loud and raucous applause.

The Dean of Durham, who also addressed the meeting, started off with conciliatory words of comfort, and highlighted the strength and unity which he believed the people of Durham had in abundance. For him, the issue of the war was what would prevail. Would it be what he referred to as the 'brutal militarism of Germany' or 'the free and self-respecting democracy of Great Britain'. Britain was after all one of the superpowers of the day and the Dean saw her as being the 'ancient guardian of human liberty', and they could not just stand by and watch whilst smaller and weaker nations were crushed underfoot and swallowed up by German imperialism. He pointed out that Germany was a very noble nation, but it was the military oligarchy who ran the country that brought shame and disgrace upon its people, a stain which he believed would eventually be its downfall.

The meeting certainly wasn't found wanting when it came to platitudes and a feeling of national pride, as these were both present in abundance. Dr John Wilson, MP, spoke at the meeting and said, 'if there was any Mad Mullah in this universe, it was a man called the German Emperor'. This sort of rhetoric was normal for the day, and almost expected. People almost needed to hear that Germany was a bad, monstrous uncontrollable beast whilst Britain and her allies were fighting for good and the freedom of civilization. Mr J.W. Hills MP told the audience that those men who were fortunate enough not to be too old, and who were free from family and domestic ties, should do their bit and enlist, in response to the request made by Lord Kitchener for 100,000 more men. By the end of the meeting a committee had been appointed, and it was decided to form a local regiment, the Durham National Emergency Volunteers.

* * *

The first real tragedy to befall Durham since the country had been at war with Germany came not in the form of somebody having being told that a loved one had been killed on the Western Front, but from the double murder of a mother and her child back home in a quiet and God-fearing neighbourhood of the city. The peaceful existence of a loving family, who were liked and well thought-of by their friends and neighbours, was sadly and dramatically shattered early one Thursday morning. Everybody was left shocked and distraught, not only at the brutality of the murders, but at who was responsible for them.

The city's coroner, Mr Cadle, held an inquest into the deaths of Mrs Annie Lancaster and her son, Robert, aged 9, who were both found dead in their home at Wheat Sheaf Yard, on Thursday, 13 August. Their throats had been cut. John Lancaster, a labourer by trade, and the husband and father of the pair, had left the house just prior to the bodies being discovered. So savage was the attack on Mrs Lancaster, that her head had almost been severed from her body.

They had lived in the three-bedroomed house, which was situated at the rear of a public house, for fourteen years. It was ascertained that Mr and Mrs Lancaster had been arguing on the morning of the murders, but generally they were described by neighbours as being a hard-working couple and not known for their arguing.

Annie's son John Richard Lancaster, affectionately known as Dick, who would have been 20 years of age at the time, had identified the bodies of both his mother and brother. Once this had been done, the coroner adjourned the inquest until Thursday, 20 August, as he said that Mr Lancaster, if he was still alive, had a right to be present to hear the evidence and ask any questions that he might have.

*Annie Lancaster.*

The events of that tragic day have been pieced together by Dick's great-grandson. Dick Lancaster left for work as usual at around six o'clock in the morning, and made his way to the nearby railway station. When he left for work, his father John was already up, getting ready to go to work himself, whilst his mother Annie was still wrapped up nice and warm in bed, cuddled up to her 9-year-old son Robert. As it turned out John didn't end up going in to work that day as he had diarrhoea, and didn't feel well enough to leave the house.

A bit later, when everyone in the house was up and about, Robert, who was known as Bobbie, his brother Herbert and sister Annie, went out to play, leaving just Annie and John at home. Sometime during the morning, Bobbie returned home on his own. At around eleven o'clock, Annie went out to buy lunch for her son Dick, who was due home at twelve noon. She was back home before 11.30 am, having purchased a meat pie from Middleton's Butchers.

At 11.45 am, a neighbour, Mrs Bridgett Delves, who lived in the next house above the Lancaster's, was going down to the yard, when she spotted Annie through her open front door. She was about to go and speak with her when she noticed John sat at the kitchen table, so she changed her mind and went about her business, calling out, 'Oh, I will see you after Mrs Lancaster.' About five minutes later, another of Annie's neighbours, a Mrs Olsen, discovered Annie's Persian kitten, which had wandered in to her house. Knowing how dear it was to her, she decided to take it back to her just in case it went missing. When she arrived at Annie's home she knocked on the door but there was no reply. She tried to open the door but it appeared to be locked. She looked through the window but could not see anybody, so went round the back to look through the kitchen window, but still couldn't see anyone, so she tapped on the window. A short while later John appeared in the kitchen and Mrs Olsen spoke to him through the closed window, and asked him to take the kitten. A short while later John opened the kitchen door and stepped out. Mrs Olsen was shocked at what she saw. John had blood smeared across his face, and in one of his hands, which was noticeably shaking, he had an open razor which was dripping with blood. John then said, 'Oh Mrs Olsen. I've cut myself whilst shaving.' He then took the kitten, went back into the house, shut the kitchen door behind him, and locked it.

Mrs Olsen was now very concerned as John had seemed somewhat agitated and the amount of blood was far too much to be consistent with somebody cutting themselves shaving. She shouted up to another neighbour, Mrs Hughes, to ask if she had seen anything of Annie, but she hadn't. Moments later another neighbour, a Mrs Delves joined Mrs Olsen in the yard. Minutes later Annie's son Dick returned home for his lunch. On seeing him walk in to the yard, Mrs Olsen ran down to him and told him to get home as quick as he could as she felt that something was wrong. Dick did as Mrs Olsen suggested, only to find the kitchen door was locked. His father suddenly opened the door to the kitchen and Dick went inside, closing the door behind him, leaving Mrs Olsen and Mrs Delves outside in the yard, still wondering what exactly was going on.

Dick was actually surprised to find his father home at that time of the day, expecting him to be away at his work.

'What are you doing home?' he asked his father.

'I don't feel well. I've got sickness and diarrhoea.' he replied.

'Where is my mother?' Dick enquired.

'She's gone out for your dinner.' John replied.

*The Lancaster family home at Wheat Sheaf Yard.*

Dick opened the back door to go and tell Mrs Olsen and Mrs Delves that his mother had gone out to get his lunch, but Mrs Olsen protested that couldn't be the case as she had seen her return home and none of the other neighbours had seen her leave the house since. Mrs Olsen advised him to go and look in the scullery. Dick agreed and asked Mrs Olsen to go with him but she refused, still scared from talking with John earlier.

Dick went back inside on his own, but left the door unlocked and open behind him. His father appeared suddenly from the back of the kitchen. 'Look at my neck.' John said. 'I have cut myself shaving.' There was a one-inch cut on the side of his neck and his hands were covered in blood. Dick could immediately sense something was wrong and that what his father was telling him simply didn't add up. He barged past his father to get to the back kitchen, who then followed behind him. At the back of the kitchen was the scullery which was separated only by a curtain. Dick moved it to one side to discover a pile of carpets and curtains which were thrown in a heap in the corner, with a bicycle strangely laid one top of the pile.

'Why are all these things piled up in the corner?' Dick shouted out, but John didn't answer, instead slipping out of the house via the back of the kitchen, rushing past Mrs Olsen and Mrs Delves, through the yard and off in the general direction of the river weir. By now Dick had started to search through the pile of curtains and carpets. He removed the bike first, followed by each of the curtains and pieces of carpet. As he removed the last piece he discovered the bodies of his mother Annie and younger brother Bobbie, lying side by side. They were totally still with blood all around them, clearly both dead. One can only try and imagine what Dick was feeling at the moment in time. Not only had he found the dead bodies of his mother and brother, but in the knowledge that the person who had extinguished their lives, was his father. How could that possibly be?

Dick thought that his father was still standing behind him in the scullery, not knowing that he had already left. Fearing for his own life he grabbed a mallet from the kitchen table, and spun around to confront him, only to discover that he wasn't there. He looked back at the carnage he had sadly discovered and could see that his mother and brother both had their throats cut. He went out into the yard and sent Mrs Olsen and Mrs Delves to get help. He then locked the door and went off to look for his father.

PC Rippon was the first police officer on the scene, arriving just after noon. Finding the door locked and unable to open it, he kicked it in and went in to the premises with Dr Vann, who had been stopped by Mrs Olsen and Mrs Delves, when he just happened to be walking by and they recognized him as a doctor. PC Rippon was soon joined by Head Constable Dunn and Detective Constable Raine. Dunn then took charge of the scene and sent Rippon and Raine off to start looking for John Lancaster. Mr Arthur Graham, the local undertaker, was the next to arrive and along with Dr Vann, he moved the two bloodied bodies into the back kitchen. Dr Vann asked Mr Graham for some water to wash the blood off of his hands, who then went to the wash stand for the basin only to find it full of bloodstained water. As he emptied it out in to the sink to refill it with clean water, a razor fell out, and this was handed to Head Constable Dunn. Another bloodstained razor was discovered in the scullery. Despite a search of the immediate area, no trace of John Lancaster was found. The search carried on throughout the Friday and Saturday, but still no sign of John was discovered.

The funerals of Annie and Bobbie took place on the afternoon of Sunday, 16 August 1914 at St Nicholas cemetery. Their bodies were taken from their humble abode, down Tilley's Yard and up the Back Lane to the awaiting hearses in Claypath, where a vast crowd, caught up in the emotion of the occasion, had gathered. Heads were uncovered and all along the route the curtains of private dwellings were drawn as marks of respect. Behind the two coffins was a procession of family members, all united in their grief, pain and shock at the loss of their loved ones in such barbaric and shocking circumstances. As they reached the cemetery, the coffins and the family were met by the vicar of St Nicholas. The cemetery's chapel was simply too small to accommodate all of those who wanted to enter, causing some to have to wait outside or around the open grave. After a brief ceremony the two coffins were lowered in to their final resting place, Annie's first followed by Bobbie's, slightly smaller in size.

At 4 am on Monday, 17 August, Sergeant Bowey and Constable Jefferson were coming to the end of a long night shift, and were patrolling by the riverside near to the old Kepier Old Mill, when they noticed an object in the river opposite Kepier Archway. Whatever it was appeared to be held stationary by something under the water. Constable Jefferson acquired a boat from nearby Kepier Lodge and they rowed out to ascertain exactly what it was that they had discovered. It was the body of John Lancaster, floating face-down in about six feet of water. They managed to release the body from its restraints and pull it in to their little boat. By the state of the body, it was clear that it had been in the water for a few days. The body was fully clothed, except for his cap and jacket. Three letters, or rather suicide notes, were found on him,. One to his son, Jimmy, one to the Coroner and a third was not legibly addressed, but none of them made absolute sense.

Whatever the problem was that led to this tragic incident, nobody was any the wiser. Everyone had only good things to say about John and Annie. Their son Dick confirmed that to his knowledge they hadn't argued with each other for several months, and even then it was not normal for them to do so. Only John and Annie know what it was that led John to act in the way in which he did on the morning of Thursday, 13 August, and sadly that is an answer which they both took to their graves with them.

The two questions which we will never know the answers to, but which are still worth posing, are would this tragedy have occurred if John had not been sick that morning and had gone to work instead and, if Annie and Herbert had come home with their brother Bobbie earlier that day, would John have slit their throats and killed them as well?

Tuesday, 18 August was a busy day. The adjourned inquest in to the deaths of Annie and Bobbie came to its conclusion. No obvious motive for the murders was discovered and the jury on delivering its verdict, came to the unsurprising conclusion that John had murdered both Annie and Bobbie and soon afterwards took his own life whilst of unsound mind. That same afternoon John's funeral took place at the same cemetery and in a grave that was adjoining his wife and son's grave. There was a large gathering at the cemetery for John's funeral despite what he had done and the tragic circumstances of his own death.

The pain and suffering of the remaining family members must have been immense. They had to deal with the tragic circumstances of all three deaths, as well as trying to comprehend the fact that their father was a murderer, but worse than all of that, there was no obvious reason why it had all happened.

Annie and John Lancaster had eleven children, three of whom had died either at birth or in their early years. Four of their sons, John (Dick), James, George and Thomas all served during the war. John Lancaster enlisted on 28 April 1915 and went on to serve as a private (M2/080835) with the Army Service Corps, and also as a private (41309) with the Lancashire Regiment. He spent time during the war in France, arriving there on 20 July 1915. He survived the war and was finally discharged on 5 March 1919.

Prior to the war James Lancaster had been a railway porter and enlisted in the Army on 22 November 1915 and was then immediately placed in the Army Reserve. He was eventually mobilized nearly three years later, on 26 August 1918, when he became a private (311305) in the Tank Corps, and was posted to the Depot Reserve Unit. Just ten days after he had been mobilized, he was admitted to the Special Division Military Hospital in Chiseldon, with an ailment that resulted in him having to spend the next twenty-eight days there. On 25

September 1919, he was posted to Ripon with the 20th Battalion, Tank Corps, in preparation for his demobilization which finally came through exactly one month later on 25 October. James married Margaret Ellen Davison on 27 July 1914 and their home address was shown as being 64 Ridley Street, in Sunderland. Their first son, James Oswald Lancaster, was born on 29 October 1914, which if the dates of the marriage and birth have been recorded correctly, would mean that Margaret was already six months pregnant when she and James were married. They had a second son, George, who was born on 19 June 1917. Interestingly enough, in James's Army Service Record, there is mention of a third son, Herbert, who was adopted: this is more than likely James's younger brother, who was orphaned after the death of his parents. His date of birth was 6 June 1907. Assuming of course Herbert hadn't already been adopted by James, prior to him marrying Margaret, he would have already been 7 years of age when they were married.

George William Lancaster enlisted in the Army and became a sapper (WR 250044) with the Railways Section of the Royal Engineers. He married Florence Mary Ryan in November 1919 in Durham.

Thomas Lancaster enlisted in the Army just four months after his eighteenth birthday, on 27 December 1916, and became a private (94478) in the 8th Battalion, Durham Light Infantry. I could not establish with any degree of certainty when exactly Thomas was demobilized, but on 14 July 1920 he in enlisted in the Territorial Force at Durham, for one year.

It was both ironic and sad that although many families suffered losses during the war, the Lancaster family experienced death in a way that they would have never dreamt of. Four sons served in the war and all of them survived, only for their mother and a younger brother to be brutally and savagely murdered, not by a stranger, but by their very own father, who also died in August 1914.

* * *

With the outbreak of war still fresh in everybody's minds, it was nice to see that sport still played an important role in everyday life.

The annual general meeting of the Durham City Rugby Football

Club took place on the evening of Thursday, 20 August at the Three Tuns Hotel. The club was in a strong financial position as it faced the beginning of another season, although those present at the meeting fully understood the implications which the war brought with it. They were not naïve and fully expected to be without many of their regular players, especially as most of their number were fit, athletic young men. If their numbers were to be depleted because of the war, then the club would survive, no matter who played in their place. Colonel Turnbill was re-elected as President, as was Councillor J.T. Boyd as Honorary Secretary and Treasurer, with Alderman H.E. Ferens as the county representative. Mr Boyd was confirmed as captain of the first team, whilst the selection of the captain of the second team could not be agreed upon in the first instance.

Cricket was on the agenda elsewhere that evening at a special meeting of the Durham Senior League, which was held in Sunderland. The purpose of the meeting was to discuss whether or not to continue with the season's fixtures, in view of the outbreak of war. After some lengthy and animated discussion, it was agreed that the season should be continued and that clubs would complete their remaining fixtures where possible. It was also agreed that a donation of £5 would be donated to the Prince of Wales' War Fund, from League funds. Only a week before the meeting, Durham had played Sunderland in a local derby. Durham had won the toss and batted first and had been bowled out for 136. Mr Milam had top scored with a knock of thirty-five. Five of the team had scored less than ten runs each, with two of those, Mr J. Darling and Mr J.H. Burrell, both bowled out for ducks.

No sooner had the war began than the desire to help those in the community who would be directly affected by the war, sprang up all over the country. Durham was no different. A meeting was held at Durham Town Hall on the evening of Tuesday, 25 August, and chaired by the Mayor, Councillor Caldcleugh, with the object of making the necessary arrangements for the local distribution in Durham of the Prince of Wales' National Relief Fund. The meeting was held in private, the outcome of which was related to the Press by the mayor.

A Central Executive Committee, with the Mayor as its chairman, had been set up and included representatives from various organizations, including public bodies, charitable organizations and local tradesmen. There were also five smaller and more local committees, which covered the areas of St Giles, St Nicholas, St Oswald, St Margaret and St Cuthbert, to ensure that anybody who might possibly have need of the fund would be not missed. It was the collective duty of these committees to investigate and decide on the merits of each and every one of the cases of distress that were brought to their attention. The mayor informed the meeting that there had been hardly any reported cases of distress in the City of Durham as a result of the war.

Even though the Durham Light Infantry was the more obvious regiment for men from Durham City to join, not everyone did so. There are possibly fifty men in a group who were photographed leaving Durham City on 3 September 1914, on route to Richmond to join the Yorkshire Regiment. The chances are that some of these men would have been work colleagues or even neighbours, and there is even more chance that not all of them survived the war.

* * *

On Thursday, 10 September, a Comrades' Battalion in the Durham County Regiment was raised. Ex-students of Bede College, Durham, sent in their names as well as the names of their comrades, so that two Bede College companies could be formed. The North-East County School, Barnard Castle, raised a company of a hundred men. Darlington had already raised one company and was looking at raising a second. Durham City raised one company. The Comrades' Battalions, like other Kitchener Battalions, had a total strength of 1,100 men. Enlistment was either for three years or for the duration of the war, whichever came first. The County of Durham not only had to raise a battalion, but had to clothe, house and train them as required by the War Office.

* * *

On Thursday, 17 September, the Borough Justices at Durham received a deputation from the Durham City Licensed Victuallers Association in reference to the hours of closing. The licensed victuallers suggested that instead of closing at 9.00 pm, as at present, the licensed houses in the city should remain open until ten o'clock in the evening and that they should remain closed until eight o'clock in the morning. Mr Bates of the Dun Cow Hotel presented the case for the trade, and the magistrates agreed that, commencing that day, that the licensed houses in the city should remain open until ten o'clock each evening, but should remain closed until eight o'clock each morning. The rule also applied to clubs as well as licensed premises.

Licensing laws had been tightened up considerably since the outbreak of the war. Munitions factories, for example, were extremely important to the war effort, because without the much-needed ammunition and artillery shells which these factories produced every single day, the war would have very quickly been lost. Men failing to turn up for work because they were either drinking in a pub, or were hungover from the previous night, was felt to be a major problem that the government had to deal with.

\* \* \*

On Friday, 2 October an article appeared in the *Newcastle Evening Chronicle* about a Durham City man who had taken part in the Battle of Mons. Corporal Bellaby of the 2nd Battalion, Coldstream Guards was wounded in the wrist during the fighting at the Battle of Mons, which took place on 23 August. If that wasn't bad enough, the next day, he and some of his comrades were trying to grab some well-earned and much needed sleep in a nearby field, when German shells suddenly began raining down amongst them, causing them to beat a hasty retreat.

Thankfully many of the shells failed to explode, which meant that Corporal Bellaby and many of his comrades were still alive who may well not have been. Two of them, a quartermaster sergeant and a company sergeant-major, were particularly fortunate when one of the German shells actually passed between them and struck the ground just a matter of feet away, but luckily for both of them failed to detonate. During the British retreat after Mons, Corporal Bellaby and his colleagues had to fight an almost constant rearguard action, as they were continually being attacked by the ever-advancing Germans, and on one occasion they even managed to shoot down an enemy aircraft.

Corporal Bellaby commented on how good and accurate the German artillery was, as well as speaking fondly of the French people,

*British soldiers in the town square at Mons.*

who stood by the side of the road holding pails of water whilst handing out fresh fruit to the British soldiers, as they hurried past. Bellaby had been given two weeks' leave and chose to come home and visit his parents who lived in Durham. After he had fully recovered from his injuries, he re-joined his regiment and returned to the fighting on the Western Front.

* * *

The war was only three months old when Durham saw a change of mayor. Councillor C. Caldcleugh stepped down to be replaced by Councillor Peter James Waite, who had being put forward by Mr W.H. Wood. That was, however, not the end of Mr Caldcleugh, who instead replaced the retiring Councillor Mr Brownless, whilst Aldermen Herring and Procter were both re-elected. In his acceptance speech, which not surprisingly included a lot about the war, he said that he felt it was the duty of every citizen to take part in some way in supporting their country in its time of need.

On the morning of Wednesday, 14 October, a party of Royal Marine Light Infantry arrived in Durham. They had just returned somewhat bedraggled from Belgium, having taken part in the defence of Antwerp. The men lived either in the City of Durham or one of the surrounding villages. They had arrived back in England the day before and had all been given seven days leave in which to visit their families. On the same day, some 200 wounded men of the Royal Naval Division, who had also fought at Antwerp, arrived at the Royal Naval Hospital at Portsmouth.

The Germans had begun bombarding Antwerp and the Belgium fortifications on 28 September with their heavy artillery. The British Royal Naval Division had begun arriving on 3 October, in an effort to support the Belgians, but on 9 October the remainder of the garrison was forced to surrender, although some Belgian and British troops did manage to make good their escape, and sought refuge in Holland, where they were interred for the rest of the war. The siege of Antwerp was a decisive victory for the Germans. The Belgians had 33,000 of their men interned in Holland, whilst a further 30,000 were captured by the Germans. British losses were fifty-seven killed, 1,480 interned in Holland and 900 taken prisoner.

\* \* \*

On the evening of Saturday, 7 November, at the Rose and Crown Hotel, in Durham City, the Secretary of the Durham County Colliery Enginemen's, Boilermakers, and Fireman's Association, Mr William Bromwell Charlton, was presented with a cheque for £100 for completing twenty-five years' service with the Association. Firstly as its president, then its treasurer, and between 1906 and 1914, its chief secretary. His wife, Mrs Charlton, was presented with a silver tea service.

The stark contrast between the evening's socializing and the merriment which went with it, for what after all, was a well-deserved presentation, was that on that same day a total of 745 British and Commonwealth officers and men were killed whilst fighting in the war. Most of these men had been in the army for no more than three months, but they had still paid the ultimate price.

It is always intriguing how attitudes change over time: one such example is in the world of Masonic Lodges. Masons most certainly do exist today, but in a less obvious and subtler kind of way. Go back in time to just over a hundred years ago, and the world of the Masons was somewhat different. In November 1914, with the war only three months old, there was a regular section in a particular newspaper, simply entitled 'Masonic Notes'. It reminded the 'Brethren' in the 'Province' of Durham, would wish to congratulate the new mayor of the City of Durham, 'Brother' P.J. Waite. Prior to having being elected as the new mayor, Mr Waite had been the 'Worshipful Master of the Marquis de Granby Lodge, the oldest lodge in the City of Durham. The author of the article spoke in the plural when he said, 'The Brethren will unite in good wishes to the Mayor and Mayoress upon attaining to the Chief civic position during a year which is certain to be one of great responsibility.' It was interesting to read of such matters so openly in a newspaper, since today Masons, although not secretive, wouldn't as a matter of course be outlining their more intimate workings in the pages of a popular daily newspaper.

\* \* \*

The Autumn Assizes for the County of Durham began in the city on Tuesday, 10 November, and were held before Mr Justice Shearman. He was accompanied by the High Sheriff of Durham, Mr Francis Priestman, the Reverend H.H. Birley as chaplain and the Under-Sheriff, Mr J.G. Wilson MA. The Grand Jury was then sworn in and consisted of twenty-two members, which included such dignitaries as Colonel J.D. Gregson, Colonel E. Leadbitter-Smith, Colonel T.C. McKenzie, Lieutenant Colonel G.F. White, Sir Hedworth Williamson, Mr Victor A. Williamson CMG, Sir John S. Barwick, and Lieutenant Colonel Hugh Bowes. With such a list of names sitting on the Jury, it almost gave a flavour of how most of the rulings were going to go as far as the scales of justice were concerned.

One of the cases to be heard at the Assizes was against Nicholaus Emil H.A. Ahlers, who was born in Hamburg in Germany, but who became a naturalized English subject in 1905, and was German consul in Sunderland. With the war only a matter of days old, Ahlers was engaged in helping young German men, who were old enough to fight, leave England and make their way back to their country where they could join the German Army and fight against Great Britain and her allies. Mr Justice Steadman raised the point about the exact wording of the statute under which Ahlers had been charged, which was very old, and dated back to the Reign of Edward III (1327–77). The statute determined that anybody was guilty of high treason who 'levies war against our Lord the King in this realm or be adherent to the King's enemies in this realm, giving to them aid and comfort in the realm or elsewhere'.

The charge of high treason was proceeded with and his trial was set for two days on 7 and 8 December. Despite protestations by Ahlers' defence that in helping young Germans escape back to Germany, he was doing so to allow them to fight against the Russians, upon whom Germany had declared war on 1 August. Ahlers' barrister, Edward Hale Tindal-Atkinson, made the preposterous claim that his client was not aware that when he provided several German men money on 4 and 5 August that Great Britain and Germany were already at war with each other.

Ahlers was found guilty of high treason and sentenced to death on 9 December. Not surprisingly, with his life in the balance, Ahlers appealed against his conviction and was acquitted and freed. Public outrage at this decision was deeply felt and emotions ran high. British and Commonwealth forces had already lost 36,273 men, killed since the war had begun, which was an average of 261 men for each and every day of the war. Against this backdrop, rioting broke out in Sunderland, and the windows of premises owned and run by Germans were smashed. Ahlers left the area soon after the trial, but he managed to cause even further outrage in May 1915, when it was discovered that rather than returning to Germany as one would have imagined, he was discovered living with his wife Emma under the assumed name of Anderson in Surbiton, Surrey. Soon after his secret had been revealed, Ahlers found himself interned in a 'concentration camp' in Islington, which had previously been the local workhouse. He remained there until the end of the war when he returned to Germany in 1919, after having his British nationality revoked. Comparisons would later be drawn between Ahlers's case and that of the British nurse Edith Cavell. She was found guilty of treason and executed by a German firing squad, in Schaerbeek in Brussels, on 12 October 1915, for helping 200 British soldiers escape from Belgium. For her there was no appeal.

Among other cases heard at the Assizes was that of Samuel Bridgett, a 26-year-old labourer, who pleaded guilty to a charge of sacrilege at Sacriston Church in Durham, on or about 3 October. He was sentenced to six months in prison. There was no explanation of what Bridgett had actually done that resulted in the charge against him, but by definition it would suggest that he either damaged a sacred object within the church or assaulted the vicar in some way.

Joseph Turnbill was a 33-year-old soldier who was charged with having stolen thirty shillings belonging to the Mayor and Corporation of Sunderland, On 26 August, in sentencing Turnbill to nine month's imprisonment, Mr Justice Shearman told him that he was of very bad character.

Caroline Hobson was a 39-year-old hawker, charged with having wounded Peter Bruce at Stockton on 2 November. Mr Paley Scot, who was prosecuting the case, explained that Bruce and Hobson had been living together. On 24 August, Bruce enlisted in the army and was sent to Grantham, but was then later discharged for being medically unfit, when he then returned to Stockton. On 2 November he found Hobson in the Red Lion Hotel. He asked her to leave and come home with him, but she refused. She eventually returned to their home later that day, in a drunken state and was somewhat excited. An argument ensued between the pair, started by her accusing him of being unfaithful, an allegation which he vehemently denied. Despite his denial, she picked up a table knife and threatened to stab him in the heart, but actually caught him in the eye, causing injury to his upper and lower eyelids, but thankfully missing the eye itself. Hobson claimed that Bruce had been provocative and struck her first with a poker, and that she only reacted in self-defence, but admitted she had consumed a good deal of whisky before returning home. Despite her protestations, the jury found her guilty of wounding and sentenced her to six months' imprisonment.

Forty-five-year-old Sarah Calvert, was accused of unlawful conversion of £54, entrusted to her by R. Thomas and Co., at South Shields, on 29 June 1912. A sea cook named Nelson went on a voyage to South America, and before leaving owed his boarding-house keeper £15 8 shillings, which in 1914, was a princely sum of money. Nelson had arranged for Calvert to receive his half-pay while he was away, pay the monies that he owed and keep the balance for him until he returned. When he eventually returned from the voyage two years later, he found that his landlord had not been paid the monies owed to him, and that Calvert had spent or couldn't account for a further £38, which she had received on his behalf. When Calvert was arrested she freely admitted receiving the money from the prosecutor, who was also the solicitor involved in the transaction, but stated that he had made no conditions as to what she should or could do with the money. The jury found her not guilty and she was discharged. This was a somewhat strange decision as regardless of what conditions the solicitor did or did not make in relation to how the money should be disposed of, she knew full well what Nelson had asked her to do with it on his behalf.

The Assizes was a court which sat at intervals in each county throughout England and Wales to administer both civil and criminal law. It had cases committed to it by the Quarter Sessions, which were local county courts. These in turn were held four times a year. The more minor offences were dealt with by Justices of the Peace in what were known as Petty Sessions. This was how the legal system remained up until the Courts Act of 1971, which saw civil matters handed over to the High Court to deal with, whilst the criminal jurisdiction was handed to the Crown Court, and became a full-time system, working on a daily basis.

* * *

A meeting of the Durham City Council took place in the Mayor's Chamber at the Town Hall, on Thursday 5 December. The meeting was presided over by the Mayor, Councillor Charles Caldecleugh. Also present was the Deputy Mayor, Councillor R. McLean, six Aldermen and sixteen other councillors.

The Mayor began the meeting by making reference to Lord Durham, who had recently lost his brother, the Honourable Francis Lambton, and his nephew, Mr Geoffrey Lambton, both of whom had been killed whilst serving in the Army in France. Lord Durham's family had a long history of military service and had family members killed and wounded in the South African (Boer) War of 1899–1902. A resolution was passed at the meeting, placing on record their appreciation for the splendid service the House of Lambton had so freely given to the country and the mayor expressed his sympathy, on behalf of all those present, for Lord Durham and his family.

Geoffrey Lambton was 26 years of age and a lieutenant in the 2nd Battalion, Coldstream Guards, when he was killed in action on 1 September 1914. He is buried at the Guards Grave in Villers-Cotterêts Forest, which is situated in the Aisne region of France. After the Allied defeat at the Battle of Mons, both the French and British forces began a long and arduous march as they retreated towards Paris. On the evening of 31 August the 4th Guards Brigade stopped north of the forest near Villers-Cotterêts, with German Army in hot pursuit. During the course of the night the Guards units had taken up entrenched defensive positions between Soucy and Mont-Gobert. The expected German attack commenced at 10 am on 1 September, with the Guards' forward positions quickly coming under heavy artillery and rifle fire, forcing elements of the Grenadier Guards, Coldstream Guards and Irish Guards to retreat into the nearby forest where the rest of their colleagues already were.

There was a particularly heavy mist that morning, and coupled with the density of the undergrowth in the forest, the German advance was greatly slowed down. Confusion reigned on that particular day, with communications extremely difficult in the circumstances. During the

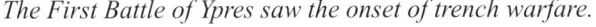

*The First Battle of Ypres saw the onset of trench warfare.*

course of the morning, many of the British units were engaged in close-quarters fighting with their German foe, which was both bloody and brutal, with men physically fighting for their very existence. By late afternoon the surviving Guardsmen had left the forest and re-joined the general retreat. Their actions that afternoon helped troops from the 2nd Division to be able to safely retreat, but their efforts had come at a heavy price, as by the end of the day more than 300 officers and men of the 4th Guards Brigade had been killed.

Geoffrey's father, The Honourable Francis Lambton, the younger brother of Lord Durham, was killed in action only a matter of weeks later. Depending on which official document one reads, different dates are shown for his death, ranging from 25 to 31 October. He was a second lieutenant in the Royal Horse Guards (The Blues) and has no known grave. His name appears on the Ypres (Menin Gate) Memorial, which is situated in the West-Vlaanderen region of Belgium. Before the war, Francis Lambton had been a racehorse trainer at Newmarket, where he lived with his father, Charles Lambton, a retired army colonel, at Bidford Cottage in Newmarket.

*The Hon. Francis Lambton. (www.roll-of-honour.com)*

\* \* \*

At their last meeting of the year, the Executive of the Durham Miners Association, remembered all of their members who had suffered in some way during the course of the year. This included the Association's General Secretary, Dr Wilson MP, who had been unwell for some time. The relatives of Captain Hugh Taylor MiD, of the 2nd Battalion, Scots Guards, were also remembered, after he was killed in action whilst serving in France on 18 December. He is buried at Le Trou Aid Post Cemetery, in the village of Fleurbaix in the Pas de Calais. Condolences were also sent to Mr Matthew Parrington, who was the agent to Monkwearmouth Coal Company, on the death of his 21-year-old son, George Bramwell Parrington, a private (2274) with the Northumberland

Hussars, who was killed in action on 25 October 1914. He has no known grave and his name is commemorated on the Ypres (Menin Gate) Memorial.

* * *

By the end of 1914, the war was already five months old. Men had been killed in their tens of thousands, causing pain and suffering to families up and down the country. The initial patriotic enthusiasm which had been in abundance at the start of the war, had started to wane somewhat, as the expected end to the war by Christmas had failed to materialize. But in the meantime, life had gone as usual. Children had been born, lovers had become engaged and married, and elderly people had passed away. Poverty was rife, the workhouse was still very much a part of a socially-unbalanced society, where literacy was still not the norm amongst the general population. Things could only get better, but the real question was how long that would take.

CHAPTER 2

# 1915
# Deepening Conflict

As the second year of the war began, nobody could have guessed at the number of battles that were destined to take place and how many lives that would be lost. On New Year's Day 1915, a grand total of 710 British and Commonwealth soldiers were killed, and on New Year's Eve, the same year, the number was 206, which brought the final number for the year, of those who had been killed, to 151,773.

Some of the more notable battles and other actions of 1915 were:

- The Battle of Dogger Bank, an engagement in the North Sea between British and German battlecruisers (24 January).
- The initial naval bombardment of the Dardanelles Straits by British warships (began 19 February).
- The Battle of Neuve Chapelle, saw 40,000 British and Indian troops, under the command of General Haig, attack German positions at Neuve Chapelle (began 10 March).
- The Second Battle of Ypres, was the only major offensive launched by the Germans against Allied forces on the Western Front throughout the whole of 1915. The battle was most notable for the Germans' use of chlorine gas for the first time. A total of 5,700 canisters, which contained some 168 tons of chlorine gas, were released on the first day, mainly against French troops (began 22 April).
- Landings at Helles and Ari Burnu (Anzac Cove) on the Gallipoli peninsula, by 35,000 Australian and New Zealand soldiers (began 25 April).

- Landings at Suvla Bay on the Gallipoli peninsula by 20,000 Australian and New Zealand troops, and more British forces arrived the next day (began 6 August).
- The Battle of Loos, a joint British and French offensive. Preceded by a four-day artillery bombardment of German positions in which 250,000 shells were fired (began 25 September).

Later in the year came the evacuation of Anzac Cove, Suvla Bay and Helles on the Gallipoli peninsula. After several weeks of indecision about whether or not to evacuate British and Commonwealth troops, Sir Ian Hamilton, the commander of the Mediterranean Expeditionary Force, was removed from his position on 14 October because he was against the idea. His replacement, Sir Charles Monro, who arrived in the peninsula on 28 October, quickly carried out a tour of the region and promptly recommended evacuation as the best resolution to the situation.

Kitchener, apparently not happy with Monro's recommendation, went to Gallipoli to see for himself what the situation was. Once he saw the conditions that the Commonwealth forces had to contend with, he changed his mind and concurred with Monro, and recommended the evacuation on 15 November, but this wasn't confirmed by the British government until 7 December.

Despite bad weather in the region, 105,000 men and 300 guns were evacuated from Suvla Bay and Anzac Cove between 10 to 20 December. The evacuation at Helles began in late December, with the safe exodus of 35,000 men.

Overall, the Gallipoli campaign had been an extremely costly affair. British and Commonwealth forces lost 59,000 killed and a further 225,000 wounded.

\* \* \*

A Rugby Union charity match was played on Saturday 2 January 1915 between the 11th Division of the Northern Army Command and the Public Schools Brigade, at the Queens Club in London. Amongst the players of the Army team were the following men from Durham: Lieutenant Arthur James Dingle, Second Lieutenant Nowell Oxland and Second Lieutenant A.E.B. Plumer. The match was a close-fought affair with the Public Schools team coming out on top, in a low-scoring game, by 12 points to 10. Dingle scored with a conversion and a try under the posts.

But this story isn't about that one rugby match but about the lives and subsequent deaths of two of those players, Nowell Oxland and Arthur James Dingle. There were numerous similarities between the two men. Nowell's father, William Oxland, was a priest. As a young man he attended Durham School before going on to Worcester College at Oxford University, to study history. As we already know, he was a keen rugby player, although his playing abilities didn't take him to quite the same level of attainment on a rugby pitch as Dingle.

*Nowell Oxland. (www.warpoets.org.uk)*

When the war began in August 1914 he was commissioned as a second lieutenant in the 6th Battalion, Border Regiment, and arrived at Gallipoli in July 1915. He took part in the landings at Suvla Bay on 6 August 1915. The next day the 6th Battalion, Border Regiment, captured Chocolate Hill. Over the course of the next couple of days they then tried to push on across 'W' Hill and onwards to Anafarta Sagir, but were unsuccessful in their attempts. It was during this action that Nowell Oxland was killed on 9 August. He was initially buried near to Chocolate Hill. Green Hill Cemetery at Suvla Bay only came into existence after the end of the war, when all of those who had been buried more or less where they fell, were disinterred and moved to Green Hill Cemetery. He was twenty-four years of age at the time of his death. Nowell Oxland became known as one of the war poets, with his best-known wartime piece being 'Outward Bound', which was printed in *The Times* shortly after his death.

Arthur James Dingle was born on 16 October 1891 at Hetton-le-Hoe, in County Durham, to Arthur Trehane and Beatrice Dingle. Arthur was a 'Cleric in Holy Orders' and the family, which also included younger son Hugh and daughters Mary and Beatrice, lived at Egglescliffe Rectory in the County of Durham.

Arthur attended Durham School before going on to study Theology at Keble College Oxford, with the intention of following his father into the priesthood. He joined the Officer Training Corps (OTC) whilst at

Oxford, and in 1911 he represented the University at Rugby Union in the Varsity match against Cambridge at the Queens Club in London on 12 December. Oxford won the match 19–0, with Dingle scoring one of the tries. Thirteen months later on 8 February 1913, he was selected to represent England in a full international match against Ireland at Lansdowne Road in Dublin. England won the match 15–4.

After Arthur had graduated from Oxford he returned to Durham, where he became a master at his old school. Early in 1914, and in effect, what was a trial match for the first full international of the year, he was selected to play for England against the South at Twickenham. England won the match 21–12. He was then selected to play for England against the Rest of the World, another match which England won, this time by a score of 42–29. He impressed sufficiently in those two games to be selected for England's third match in that season's Five Nations competition on 21 March 1914, against Scotland at Inverleith on a cold windy day, which England won 16–15, in a very close match, in part due to having to play part of the game with fourteen men, after one of their players sustained a broken leg. This was England's last match on British soil before the outbreak of the First World War. Sadly, by the end of 1918, eleven of the thirty men who played in that match were dead, victims of the war. Dingle was also selected for the final match of that season's Five Nations, against France at Colombes on 13 April 1914, with England coming out commanding winners by 39–13. This victory rounded off a fantastic season for England, who in the process won the Calcutta Cup, beating Scotland, as well as the Triple Crown and the Five Nations Championship.

Once the war had started, all competitive rugby matches were suspended, but Edgar Mobbs, who himself represented England on seven occasions between 1909 and 1910, organized a match between the Barbarians and the Royal Army Medical Corps. After a tight first half, the match was still evenly balanced at 0–0, but in the second half, the Barbarians had the better of the play and ran out winners by a score of 10–3. Two of Dingles teammates that day, Edgar Hobbs and Billy Green, both fellow England internationals, were killed during the war.

As a schoolmaster, Dingle was exempt from military service, but he volunteered nonetheless. He had been instrumental in setting up the OTC at Durham School and hadn't thought of not serving his country. With the war nearly a month old, he received a commission on 29

August, as a second lieutenant in the 6th Battalion, East Yorkshire Regiment.

On 6 August 1915, the Allied landings took place at Suvla Bay, on Gallipoli, and on 9 August the 6th Battalion took their objective by capturing Scimitar Hill, but lost 137 of their men in doing so. Having captured the hill, the East Yorkshire Regiment then made a tactical withdrawal. On 21 August the 6th Battalion were once again involved in fighting for Scimitar Hill after the decision had been made to retake the hill.

It has to be remembered that Dingle was still only twenty-three years of age, still a comparatively young man, who had already crammed so much in to his few years.

Dingle, who had been promoted to the rank of temporary captain on 9 August, was the acting commanding officer of the 150 men of 'B' Company of the 6th Battalion, when the Battle of Scimitar Hill began on 21 August. Whilst defending a captured Turkish trench against overwhelming numbers of enemy troops, Dingle was shot and killed, at dawn on 22 August. His body was never recovered.

Arthur James Dingle was later immortalized, in part of a poem written by John Still, entitled 'The Ballad of Suvla Bay'.

*Arthur James Dingle. (Wikipedia – unknown author)*

> James Dingle
> Broad, and simple, and great of heart,
> Strenuous soul in a stalwart frame;
> Whatever the work, he took his part,
> With energy strung from the very start
> To learn the rules and play the game.
>
> He played for an English side before;
> And all unspoiled by the crowd's applause,
> He took for his side their greeting roar:
> And so in the greater game of war
> He gave his life for the greater cause.

Arthur Dingle is commemorated on a memorial at Durham School as well as another at St Margaret's Church in Durham. His younger brother, Hugh John Dingle, was a Probationary Surgeon in the Royal Naval Volunteer Reserve, and was on board HMS *Petard* at the Battle of Jutland on 31 May 1916, when he was killed in action. He was twenty-three years of age and is buried at Queensferry Cemetery in West Lothian, Scotland.

In the space of just nine months Reverend Arthur Trehane Dingle and his wife, Beatrice, had lost both of their sons. One wonders if Arthur ever lost his faith and how he reconciled their sad loss with his deeply-held religious beliefs. When he died on 28 June 1952, he was still a serving priest.

\* \* \*

The New Year didn't start off very well in Durham, with reports of two drownings in the River Wear. This followed the death on New Year's Eve of a six-year-old local boy, Arthur Davis, who lived in Framwellgate. He fell into the river by the gas works, and was swept away before anybody could go to his rescue.

In the early hours of Saturday 2 January, the body of Mrs Florence Gibson, a resident of Framwellgate and who was married to Michael, who worked as a stoker at the Durham Gas Works, was recovered from the River Wear, by local resident, Daniel Sharks, who just happened to be walking by when he spotted her body floating in the river. Her baby was believed to have drowned with her, but her body was not recovered.

On 21 December Mrs Gibson was seen by her doctor at home. She was last seen alive in the kitchen of her property by her husband, Michael, at about ten o'clock in the evening on New Year's Day, when she appeared fine. He woke up at about 3.30 the following morning, to discover both his wife and baby were not there. He immediately went to see his mother-in-law, who lived in the same street, to see if she was there, but she was not.

Michael and Florence lived at 39 Framwellgate, Durham. The census of 1911, showed that one of their two children, had already died before this date, and that the other, daughter Florence, was one year, nine months of age. Four years later she would have been nearly six years of age, hardly a baby as described in the Press, so maybe Michael and Florence had a third child who was born after this time, and was the one reported to have drowned with Florence in 1915.

* * *

Arthur Duncombe Shafto was a holder of the Distinguished Service Order and a captain in 'D' Company, 2nd Battalion, Royal Scots, when he was killed in action on 26 August during the Battle of Le Cateau, although the British Army's First World War Medal Roll index cards record his date of death as being 12 September 1914. He was thirty-four years of age and is buried at the Caudry British Cemetery, which is situated in the Nord region of France, not far from the town of Cambrai. He left a widow, Marguerite Cecile Catherine.

The town of Caudry saw fighting during the Battle of Le Cateau and remained in German hands until October 1918, but for the most part it was a centre for German medical units. This carried on when it was eventually captured by the British 37th Division, and was then used by a series of casualty clearing stations. The following information is taken from the Commonwealth War Graves Commission entry for the Caudry British Cemetery.

> The British Cemetery, originally called the German Cemetery Extension, was begun in October 1918 by the New Zealand Division and carried on by the Casualty Clearing Stations. It was completed after the Armistice by the concentration of graves from the German Cemetery as well as the Audencourt British Cemetery, which lay between the villages of Audencourt and Beaumont, in the middle of fields. It was made by the Germans after the Battle of Le Cateau, and Plot 1 contained the graves of 66 soldiers from the United Kingdom, mainly of the 2nd Battalion, Royal Scots and the 1st Battalion, Gordon's, who fell in that battle.

Captain Shafto's family placed a memorial to commemorate him in St Margaret's Church in Durham. It was in the form of a black cross with a marble background, and placed in the base of the west window. There is a certain sad irony when one discovers another tablet on the north wall of the church, offering thanks to God for the preservation of

Arthur's life during his service in the war in South Africa. This sits alongside another tablet, which was in memory of his brother who was killed in the same war.

Thomas Dunscombe Shafto, a cousin of Arthur's, was a captain in the Royal Fusiliers (London Regiment) when he was killed whilst serving in the Dardanelles, on 2 May 1915. He is buried in the Redoubt Cemetery in Helles, on the Gallipoli Peninsula. No sooner had the family remembered the loss of Arthur, than they were back at St Margaret's Church, commemorating the sad loss of his father, Charles Ottiwell Duncombe Shafto, who died at 4.30 am on Friday 22 January of peritonitis, after catching a chill whilst out walking with a friend two days previously. Mr Shafto was widely known throughout the town, and a very well-respected individual. Two years earlier, he had undergone an extremely serious operation, which he had never fully recovered from.

Mr Shafto was born in 1853, and at the age of ten, he entered Durham School, where he stayed for the next ten years. His next stop on the academic ladder was as a scholar at Jesus College Cambridge, where he studied Classics. During his time at both Durham and Cambridge, he became a very proficient oarsman, captaining the 'fours, pairs and eights' as a University rower. He was part of the Cambridge team in 1876 that beat the Oxford Crew by six lengths in the Boat Race and the following year he rowed for Cambridge again, and this time it was a dead heat.

He left Cambridge in 1878, studied as a barrister and was called to the Bar at the Inner Temple in London and then served for several years on the North-Eastern Circuit, before failing eyesight caused him to retire, when he then became a country gentleman, residing at Wolsingham, Mainsforth Hall and in 1905, moved in to 9 South Bailey.

In 1877 he had married Helena Rosa Wilkinson, the daughter of Reverend G.P. Wilkinson, who at one time had been the Vice-Chairman of the Durham Quarter Sessions, and the brother of Bishop Wilkinson, who was the Bishop of Hexham and Newcastle.

Mr Shafto was a regular churchgoer as was the fashion of the day, but he did much valuable work for the parish of St Margaret's which he had been associated with for many years. He was a sidesman and a member of the Select '24'. A sidesman is more commonly known as a church usher, and his duties consist of welcoming members of the congregation in to the church, seating arrangements and taking the collection.

Politically, he was a staunch Conservative and a prominent member of the Durham Constitutional Association, taking an active part in the organization, even including his wife and daughter who were active workers in the local branch of the Primrose League. During his time, Mr Shafto, was regular in his attendance as a Magistrate at Durham County Police Court and had also been a member of the Durham City and County, Councils.

* * *

Christmas time, and especially Christmas Day, has always held an appropriate place in the hearts and minds of most Christian people, and the war years had made the yearly celebrations prophetic for most. For some it was no longer a time of rejoicing, but a time of remembering a loved one, lost in the war, but either way Christmas time brought people together in a religious sense, the focal point of which was the church.

As usual, Christmas Day in Durham City was devoted primarily to attending mass, although for some that was at midnight on Christmas Eve, rather than on Christmas Day morning. But being a cathedral city, the main celebration mass was always going to be the latter. A memorable service was held at Durham Cathedral in 1914, with a notable sermon delivered by Dean Henson on the paradox of Christianity, which was particularly poignant in the circumstances. An individual's faith was always likely to be challenged at such times, but Dean Henson understood that. It didn't take a genius to work out that losing a loved one in a war could result in people questioning their faith and beliefs. With this in mind, his sermon contained varied content about the war and its different aspects, and played a large part of what he had to say.

As in previous years the carol services in the Cathedral were once again extremely popular. Christmas Day, Boxing Day and the Tuesday, saw carols sung by the choir, and at each service, the Dean delivered an appropriate discourse.

* * *

Many men from the parish of St Margaret's in Durham City enlisted in the military during the course of the First World War, as soldiers, sailors or airmen, and by February 1915, several of them had already been killed in the fighting. The Rector of St Margarets, the Reverend Ralph Watson, was keen that their names should be remembered and not forgotten.

Arthur Duncombe **Shafto** and the circumstances surrounding his death were covered earlier in this chapter.

Percy **Buckle**. The Commonwealth War Graves Commission website only shows a Percival Buckle, who was a rifleman in the West Yorkshire Regiment (Prince of Wales Own), but he wasn't killed until 9 October 1917.

Hugh John Sladen **Shields** was a Lieutenant in the Royal Army Medical Corps, attached to the 1st Battalion, Irish Guards, when he was killed in action on either 26 October 1914. His body was never recovered and his name is commemorated on the Ypres (Menin Gate) Memorial. Shields was born in Calcutta, India on 16 June 1887, to Arthur John and Mary Forbes, and had been gazetted as a lieutenant in the Royal Army Medical Corps on 26 July 1912, two years before the war began. When war broke out he was initially under orders to proceed to India, but instead he left for France on 12 August 1914. He saw his first action on 23 October 1914 and three days later he was dead.

*Hugh John Sladen Shields.*

His commanding officer, Lord Ardee, wrote of him:

> He was killed while attending to a wounded man in the firing line during an attack on Rentel, eight to ten miles east of Ypres. I cannot say how much we all sympathize with your loss and how much we feel it ourselves. The way in which he insisted on attending to wounded men under fire was the admiration of all of us. On more than one occasion I have advised him not expose himself so much, but he always would do it, out of a sense of duty. He was shot in the mouth and through the neck while bending down and was killed instantly.

Another officer described what happened:

> The Battalion were in action in the Polygon Wood four and a half miles due east of Ypres. There were two companies in reserve, two in the main line of trenches, and a few outposts, which is rather a risky job unless there is good cover. Needless to say, the usual place of medical officers is with reserves or further back. On this occasion the cover for the outposts was rotten. They were fairly along like caterpillars under rather a bad fire, till one of them was laid out, and lay there in the open thrashing about. Orr Ewing of the Scots Guards, at present commanding us, said at dinner the other night that he was appalled to see Shields strolling out across our trenches (all our men in the trenches with their heads down), and go and fish out some bandages and tie him up. Needless to say he was hit before he had been there one moment; the shot hit him in the neck and killed him outright.

Captain the Hon. H. Alexander also wrote of Shields.

> I think the nicest thing I ever heard was said by one of our men, who said, 'Mr Shields is the bravest man I ever saw.' The officers said he was too brave and told him, but he always said he felt it was his duty to help wounded men whenever he could. If anyone has done his duty and a great deal more, he has. He was with us all the time up to Villers-Cotterêts, where he stayed behind with the wounded and was taken by the Germans, that was 1 September. He re-joined us again at Soupir. It was here that we went up the Castle together. It was at Soupir where Hugh did such frightfully good work by carrying the wounded, both English and German, out of a burning farm which was being heavily shelled. We moved up from there about 20 October to Ypres. Hugh died in front of a place called Roulers; he was attending to a wounded man in the open during an attack not more than 200 yards from the enemy. We are all very sorry, as he was so popular in my regiment, but there is consolation in the thought that he himself would not have wished a better death, and he could not have died more gallantly.

He was mentioned in Despatches by Field Marshal Sir John French in the *London Gazette* on 19 October 1914 for gallant and distinguished service in the field, and recommended for the Victoria Cross by his brigadier, Lord Cavan, but despite his commanding officer's high rank and lofty position in society, no such award was ever made.

He was buried, soon after his death, in the grounds of Huize Beckenhorst, Zillibeke. It can only be assumed that somewhere during the course of the war Hugh's grave was lost, or destroyed by an artillery bombardment, as his name is recorded on the Ypres (Menin Gate) Memorial, which indicates that he now has no known grave.

John Mounsey **Lambert**, a captain in the 3rd (Reserve) Battalion attached to the 1st Battalion, Northumberland Fusiliers, was born on 21 December 1883, in Alnwickand. He had enlisted in Northumberland in 1903, and become a second lieutenant on 3 July 1905. He was further promoted to the rank of lieutenant 1 November 1906 and then to captain on 29 August 1914. He was killed in action on 27 October 1914 during the Battle of Neuve Chapelle, and is buried at the Caberet-Rouge British Cemetery at Souchez, which is situated in the Pas de Calais region of France. He was the son of the late Major-General George Craster Lambert, who had served with the 101st Royal Bengal Fusiliers.

John William **Scarth** was born in Durham on 27 February 1895, and was one of John and Annie Scarth's seven children. The family lived at 10 Prospect Terrace, Neville's Cross, Durham. He enlisted on 15 April 1914, four months before the outbreak of the war, in the 1st Battalion, Coldstream Guards as a private (10683). He had previously served as an able seaman in the Royal Navy, before transferring to the Army. He was killed in action on 15 November 1914 and is buried at the Boulogne Eastern Cemetery, in the Pas de Calais region of France.

*John William Scarth.*

John had two brothers who both served in the First World War and survived. They were Thomas Atkinson Scarth and Charles Henry Scarth. Thomas was born in Durham in 1891 and when he left school, like most local young men, he became a coal miner. He enlisted in the Army on 5 August 1913 at Sunderland, becoming a private (41990) in the 20th Hussars. He was twenty-two years of age at the time, and he signed on for twelve years, which meant serving five years with the Colours before then spending a further seven years in the Army Reserve. His basic training began at Scarborough on 7 August 1913, but his military service was nearly over before it had begun, when after having undergone his Army medical examination at Scarborough Military Hospital, a decision was made that Thomas wasn't likely to become an efficient soldier, but there was no explanation attached on his Army service record as to why. The letter dated 9 August 1913, which had been sent by the captain commanding the Northern Cavalry Depot, was sent to the Deputy Director of Medical Services, Northern Command in York. On 3 September 1913 a Lieutenant Colonel R. Copeland with the Royal Army Medical Corps, who was charge of the Medical Inspections of new recruits, replied to the Officer Commanding the Northern Cavalry Depot as follows: 'Forms B178 & B265 of Pte Scarth 20 Hussars returned herewith. As this recruit's physique is good, he can be retained in the service.' He arrived in France as part of the British Expeditionary Force on 19 May 1915 and was attached to the 5th Battalion, Machine Gun Corps on 25 February 1916 before being transferred to them permanently just over three months later on 9 June. He remained in France until 12 August 1918 before returning to England to have his wounds treated, having served in France for three years and eighty-six days.

His disciplinary record showed two incidents, exactly one year apart. The first took place on 22 January 1917, when he was charged with two offences, disobedience of orders and of being improperly dressed on exercise. He was found guilty on both charges, and docked seven days' pay. The second offence happened on 22 January 1918, when he was charged with neglect of duty whilst on sentry, by failing to report a horse badly injured. He was found guilty of this offence and docked ten days' pay.

He was discharged from the Army on 3 December 1918 as no longer being physically fit enough for war service, due to a gunshot wound to his left arm, which was going to prevent him from carry out his duties for at least six months. He had served for five years and 121 days. He was awarded the 1914–15 Star, the Victory Medal and the British War Medal as well as a weekly pension of 13 shillings and 9 pence, which was to be reviewed after fifty-two weeks.

46  DURHAM CITY IN THE GREAT WAR

*The King's Certificate.*

On 19 September 1919, Thomas was awarded the King's Certificate (R 10064/18). Any man who had served in His Majesty's armed forces and had been discharged as a result of having been wounded and disabled was awarded this. It came with a silver war badge which had an individual serial number, which if lost, could not be replaced. It was to then be worn by the recipient on their civilian clothes, so that others would immediately know that they had served during the war, and were not a coward. Although first issued in 1916, it was also retrospectively awarded to all of those who had been medically discharged through disability since the beginning of the war.

Charles Henry Scarth was born on 14 April 1899. When the war started he was still only fifteen years of age. When he was old enough he followed his brothers into the Army. He was attested on 20 February 1917 in Newcastle-upon-Tyne, immediately placed in the Army Reserve, and then two months later on 30 April 1917, he was called up aged eighteen years. Like his brothers Thomas and John, before enlisting he had worked in one of the local mines, where because of his age he was employed as a shaft lad. He became a private (60548) in the 3rd Battalion, West Yorkshire Regiment, and whilst in France as part of the British Expeditionary Force, he was diagnosed with tonsillitis. He was treated at No. 26 Casualty Clearing Station on 16 April 1918. The next day he was treated at No. 6 General Hospital at Rouen, and although the documents are not totally legible, it appears to show that he returned to England on 27 April 1918. Further down the page on the same document, it clearly shows that he arrived back in England on 29 October 1918 and was posted to the 15th/17th Battalion West Yorkshire Regiment and on 2 November 1918 he was posted again, this time to the 10th Battalion of the same regiment.

His service record then becomes slightly confusing as it also shows him as having been in hospital at the 3rd Scottish General Hospital, which before the war had been the Stobhill Hospital in Glasgow, but in 1914 it was requisitioned by the Royal Army Medical Corps and became the 3rd and 4th Scottish Hospitals. It had originally been opened in 1904. He was there from 29 April 1918 for a period of thirty days, at which time it would appear that he was then transferred to Kings Lancashire Military Convalescent Hospital in Blackpool on 30 May, where he remained until 13 June, by which time his condition had improved. The only conclusion I can come to is that after he was released from hospital in June 1918 he returned to France, before then returning to England on 29 October.

Ernest Geoffrey **Cadle** was a sixteen-year-old midshipman serving on board HMS *Formidable* when she was sunk whilst on an exercise in the English Channel on New Year's Day 1915, making him one of the youngest, if not the youngest, individual from Durham, to have been killed whilst serving in the armed forces during the First World War. His parents, Charles and Elizabeth Cadle, lived at 26 North Bailey, Durham. The *Formidable* was struck by two torpedoes fired by the

H.M.S. FORMIDABLE.
THIS ILL-FATED BATTLESHIP SANK IN THE ENGLISH CHANNEL AFTER A TERRIBLE EXPLOSION IN THE EARLY MORNING OF 1st JANUARY, 1915. A TERRIBLE GALE WAS RAGING, AND ONLY 199 OF OUR BRAVE SAILORS WERE SAVED OUT OF ABOUT 750. THE GALLANT CAPTAIN BEING AMONGST THE DROWNED.

*HMS* Formidable. *(Wikipedia)*

German submarine *U-24*, which struck one of the ship's boiler rooms on her port side. As a result, a total of thirty-five officers and 512 men from the *Formidable,* including Ernest, lost their lives.

Cyril Gordon **Hosking** was a lieutenant in the 4th Squadron, Royal Flying Corps, as well as the 102nd Battery, Royal Field Artillery, when he was killed on 26 October 1914, whilst flying over Ypres. His brother Herbert Hosking, who was thirty-one years of age and a captain, serving with the 66th Punjabis, also died during the war. He was killed in action during the relief of Kut in Mesopotamia, on 3 February 1917, and is buried in the Amara War Cemetery in Iraq. Cyril, was born in India, one of ten children of Edward and Annette Hosking, on 30 July 1890. Edward, who was a judge in the Indian Civil Service, died on 30 July 1890, which resulted in Annette bringing her children back to England and settling in Oxford. One of his sisters, Emily May Hosking, married Major Edward Gonville Bromhead on 6 November 1897, who was related to Gonville Bromhead, who won famously won a Victoria Cross for his actions at Rorke's Drift on 22 and 23 January 1879.

Arthur **Vest** was just eighteen years of age and a private (10148) in the 1st Battalion, East Yorkshire Regiment, when he was killed in

1915: DEEPENING CONFLICT   49

action on 20 October 1914. His body was never recovered and his name is commemorated on the Ploegsteert Memorial, which is situated in the Hainaut region of Belgium. His parents, John and Isabella Vest lived at 39 Atherton Street, Durham.

February 1915 saw the death of Charles Stewart **Vane-Tempest-Stewart**, the 6th Marquis of Londonderry, a resident of Durham for

*The Marquess of Londonderry. (Portrait by John Singer Sargent)*

many years, as well as one of the City's distinguished Freemen. The honour had been accorded to his lordship, together with the Earl of Durham, in 1912, both noblemen having, in a variety of ways, rendered service to the county town. In 1911, Lord Londonderry was the Mayor of Durham and during his tenure performed many notable acts, including the opening of the extensive sewage works as well as an extension to St Hilda's College. He also conducted the opening ceremony of the City's Bowling Green.

He had led an interesting and varied life. After his father's death in 1884 he became the Lord Lieutenant of Ireland between 1886 and 1889. He was a landowner, coal-owner in County Durham and benefactor, as well as a Conservative politician, for whom he served in numerous capacities, including that of Postmaster General between 1900 and 1902 and the President of the Board of Education between 1902 and 1905. He had also held the positions of Deputy Lieutenant of Montgomeryshire and County Durham and was a Justice of the Peace for the County of Durham.

He was a supporter of the Protestant cause in Ulster and was against the very idea of Irish Home Rule. Along with 113 other Conservative politicians he voted against the Parliament Act of 1911, which in essence sought to reduce the powers which the House of Lords had over the House of Commons, by reducing its power to block legislation. A portrait of Lord Londonderry was hung in a prominent position on one of the walls of Durham Town Hall, along with those of other distinguished gentlemen from across the years.

* * *

The following is a Nominal Roll of all officers from the 8th Battalion, Durham Light Infantry, who embarked at Folkestone on 19 April 1915, as per the battalion's war diaries.

Lieutenant Colonel J. Turnbull
Captain F.G. Harvey
Captain J.A. Bradford
Captain J.A.S. Ritson
Captain E.H. Veitch
Captain W.H. Coulson

Captain J. Turnbull
Lieutenant G.E. Blackett
Lieutenant P. Kirkup
Lieutenant J.L. Wood
Lieutenant W. Johnson
Lieutenant E.A. Leybourne
Lieutenant J.R. Brass
Lieutenant W. Marshall
Second Lieutenant C.W. Baldwin
Second Lieutenant J.N.O. Rogers
Second Lieutenant T.W. Callinan
Second Lieutenant F.W. Weeks
Second Lieutenant A.W. Hisbith
Second Lieutenant J.O. Wilson
Second Lieutenant C.L.B. Whall
Second Lieutenant B.H. Richardson
Captain and Adjutant G.A. Stevens (Royal Fusiliers)
Lieutenant & Quartermaster W. Francis
Lieutenant J.A. Stenhouse (Royal Army Medical Corps)

The following four officers were killed or subsequently died of their wounds as a result the fighting which took place between 24 and 26 April 1915. Thomas William **Callinan** was born in Durham City in 1893, the son of the late Reverend Thomas and Mrs J.M. Callinan of 7 Western Hill, Durham. Part of his education saw him attend the Durham School, where he was captain of the rugby team. From there he went on to study at Queens College, at Cambridge University, graduating from there in 1905 with a degree in Classic Honours. He became a schoolmaster, taking up different posts before in 1912, ending up at the Old Merchant's Taylor's School, teaching Modern Languages. Whilst there he enrolled in the school's OTC, and at the outbreak of the war he joined the Durham Light Infantry.

*Thomas William Callinan.*

After completing his basic training, he arrived in France on 19 April 1915 and was killed in action on 25 April 1915, only six days later.

Initially he was reported as having been wounded, then in July 1915, that status was changed to wounded and missing and then in early August 1915, he was officially listed dead. He left a widow Josephine, who lived at 5 Laburnum Avenue, Durham. He has no known grave and his name is commemorated on Ypres (Menin Gate) Memorial.

James Robson **Brass** was a lieutenant who was killed on the night of 26/27 April 1915. He was twenty-four years of age at the time of his death. He is buried at the Potijze Burial Ground Cemetery, in West Vlaanderen in Belgum. His parents, Thomas and Mary Jane Brass, lived at Charlaw House, Sacriston, Durham.

William **Marshall** was a lieutenant when he was killed on 27 April 1915. He has no known grave but his name is commemorated on the Ypres Menin Gate Memorial.

Basil Hutton **Richardson** was a nineteen-year-old second lieutenant when he died on 31 May 1915. His father, Mr R Morris, lived in Newcastle. He is buried at Neiderzwehren Cemetery in Kassel, in the Hessen region of Germany. This is a strong indication that Basil had been held as a prisoner of war by the Germans that and sadly he died whilst in captivity.

The following officers were initially reported as having been wounded:

Major J.R. Ritson
Captain F.G. Harvey
Lieutenant E.A. Leybourne
Second Lieutenant F.W. Weeks
Lieutenant & Quartermaster W.G. Francis
Second Lieutenant Motum
Lieutenant J.A. Stenhouse Royal Army Medical Corps
Second Lieutenant A.W. Hisbith

The last two men were initially reported as being missing

For these three days of fighting between 24 and 26 April 1915, and excluded the figures shown above in relation to the officers, the 8th Battalion, Durham Light Infantry lost eight-one men killed, 153 wounded and a staggering 340 reported missing.

An interesting footnote of these three days in April 1915, was that some twelve years after the event, 4 February 1927, letters and reports

1915: DEEPENING CONFLICT   53

of what happened at Gravenstafel Ridge were still being written about by the officers who had been involved in it. Why these detailed written accounts of the events were required twelve years after they had taken place, is not known.

* * *

Although not born in Durham City, but County Durham, I felt Thomas Kenny's remarkable story still warranted a mention in these pages. A steely determination shown by a man who was just not prepared to leave a colleague and a fellow human being, laying wounded in the middle of no man's land.

Thomas Kenny was born in South Wingate on 4 April 1882, to Darby and Mary Kenny. He had a younger brother, John, and two sisters, Annie and Winifred. In the 1891 Census the family were living in Hutton Henry and Thomas was only nine years of age. At the outbreak of the First World War, he was already thirty-two years of age and prior to this he had been a miner at the South Wingate Pit, in the town where he lived.

He enlisted in the Army in late 1914 and became a lance sergeant (17424) in the 13th Battalion, Durham Light Infantry, first arriving in France on 25 August 1915. He was involved in fighting at La Houssoie on 4 November 1915, when he performed an act of bravery which won him the Victoria Cross.

*Thomas Kenny, from a cigarette card.*

The award of the Victoria Cross to Kenny was announced in the *London Gazette* on Tuesday, 7 December 1915. It read as follows:

Private 17424 Private Thomas Kenny, 13th (Service) Battalion, The Durham Light Infantry.

For most conspicuous bravery and devotion to duty on the night of 4th November, 1915, near La Houssoie.

When on patrol in a thick fog with Lieutenant Brown, 13th Battalion, Durham Light Infantry, some Germans, who were lying out in a ditch in front of their parapet opened fire and shot Lieutenant Brown through both thighs. Private Kenny, although heavily and repeatedly fired upon, crawled about for more than an hour with his wounded officer on his back, trying to find his way through the fog to our own trenches. He refused more than once to go on alone, although told by Lieutenant Brown to do so. At last when utterly exhausted, he came to a ditch which he recognized, placed Lieutenant Brown in it, and went back to look for help. He found an officer, and a few men of his battalion at a listening post, and after guiding them back, with their assistance Lieutenant Brown was brought in, although the Germans again opened heavy fire with rifles and machine guns, and threw bombs [i.e. hand grenades] at 30 yards distance. Private Kenny's pluck, endurance and devotion to duty, were beyond praise.

The officer who returned with Thomas Kenny to where he had left Lieutenant Brown, was Captain White. For his efforts that day in the rescue of his fellow officer, White was awarded the Military Cross. Sadly, and despite Private Kenny's best efforts, Lieutenant Philip Anthony Brown later died of his wounds. He was twenty-nine years of age.

Philip Anthony Brown was born on 27 January 1886 far away from Durham City, in fact he hailed from the other end of the country at Beckenham in Kent. He attended Oxford University where he gained a first-class degree in Modern History. He took up literary work, and for a period of time, lectured at the London School of Economics, later becoming a lecturer in Economics at Durham University. He took a particular interest in the education of working-class men and women, and became a tutor in the Workers Educational Association.

*Philip Anthony Brown.*

A month into the war he made the decision to join up and enlisted as a private in the 6th Battalion, Durham Light Infantry. He was then commissioned as a second lieutenant into the 13th Battalion, Durham Light Infantry on 13 October. He was promoted to lieutenant and on 3 February 1915, and made an assistant adjutant. He arrived in France in August 1915, before being killed three months later on 4 November. He was initially buried at La Guernerie, near Bois Grenier, but after the Armistice his grave, along with those of other British soldiers, were moved to what is now known as Ration Farm New Military Cemetery, which is situated south of the village of La Chapelle-d'Armentières. A colonel of the Durham Light Infantry wrote of him: 'He was the most popular officer with both officers and men in the Regiment, and his platoon were so angry that they could with difficulty be restrained from going out then and there to avenge his death.'

Thomas Kenny survived the war and after he returned home went back to his old job as a miner. On 29 November 1948, with Thomas now sixty-six years of age, and still working, he was killed in an accident at South Wingate Pit. He was survived by his wife Isabel, and their four children, Olive, Isabel, Annie and baby son John. He is buried at Wheatley Hill Cemetery.

CHAPTER 3

# 1916
# The Realization

❖

The war hadn't ended by the Christmas of 1914, as everybody said it would. The world was in exactly the same situation a year later: Christmas came and went in 1915, and still there was a war going on. The expectation of it being over any time soon, had long ago dissipated as no more than a dream.

Two bloody battles would take place during the course of 1916, which would ultimately have a telling effect on the outcome of the war. The first was the Battle of Verdun, but most historians see the second, the Battle of the Somme, as an Allied victory, but the real discussion point is whether or not the price that was paid, in suffering and the loss of human life, was too high. In other words, did the end justify the means?

The Battle of Verdun saw the Germans pitted against the French. By the time the battle was over, nearly 600,000 men had become casualties. The battle had commenced on 21 February with a bombardment by approximately 1,200 German heavy guns, the battle and the almost senseless waste of human life did not end until 14 July, when the Germans finally called off their offensive.

The battle had begun with some initial German gains, both in territory and objectives taken, but the French fought and defended doggedly and resolutely, determined not to lose. After all, national pride was at stake and France was just not prepared to roll over and let Germany have it all their own way.

The Battle of the Somme began on 1 July 1916 and lasted for over four months. It was between German forces and ten of the Allied nations. British and French forces fought alongside those from Australia, Canada, New Zealand, India, Newfoundland, Bermuda, Southern Rhodesia and South Africa. After the fighting was finished, the Allies had seen a total of 794,238 casualties. An estimated 50,000 of these were incurred on the very first day. Of those, 20,000 were killed. In Haig's diary for 1 July 1916, there was an entry which in essence said, that taking in to account the length of the front they had attacked along, coupled with the size of the enemy force they were up against, the number of casualties that had been sustained wasn't that bad. Looking at that through today's eyes, it appears extremely callous, cold-hearted in fact, with little or no compassion towards the men under his command.

Arguably a lot of the tactics employed throughout the war, on both sides, were outdated. They were from a different era. Whilst weaponry had greatly improved in such areas as machine guns, tanks and heavy artillery, tactics most definitely hadn't. The combination of the two opposites resulted, in part, in the excessively large numbers of soldiers who were killed and wounded. A lot of the senior officers who were in charge of the armies in the First World War, were old and had learnt their tactics twenty and thirty years before, tactics which had no place in modern warfare. There was an element of arrogance amongst some of the senior officers, who saw the men under their command, certainly not as equals and in some cases as collateral damage in their pursuit of the greater good. The German casualties for the Battle of the Somme are reported as being 537,918. The Somme campaign was broken up into three phases. Phase 1 lasted from 1–17 July, and incorporated three battles. Phase 2 lasted from July to September and consisted of four smaller battles, whilst the third and final stage, lasted from September to November and was made up of six battles.

On the home front the Military Service Act, which made all single men aged between eighteen and forty-one liable for conscription, was passed. The Act had been brought in because men were not voluntarily enlisting in the numbers which had been hoped they would, whilst the numbers of men who had already been killed and wounded continued to increase. Despite poster campaigns, attempts at persuasion that encouraged men to enlist in the armed forces, and a reliance on patriotic fervour, there were still insufficient numbers of men in uniform. The simple fact for the government and the military top brass was that they needed more men to win the war. To even consider the possibility of losing the war was inconceivable.

This was the situation which Durham found itself having to contend with during 1916, but despite all of this, life had to go on as normally as it possibly could.

During the First World War, the Durham Light Infantry managed to raise a grand total of forty-three battalions, which was an amazing achievement. This included four battalions of the Regular Army, eighteen battalions with the Territorial Force, fourteen of the New Armies, and seven other battalions. Of these, the following were raised in Durham: the 1st/8th (Service) Battalion in August 1914, the 16th (Reserve) Battalion on 10 April 1915 and the 19th (Service) Battalion, which was formed on 13 January 1915.

Not all men who joined the Durham Light Infantry were born and bred in either the county or the city but they all still fought and served under the name of Durham. During 1916, a total of 3,507 men of the Durham Light Infantry were killed or died as a result of active service. Of these 208 were serving with the 1st/8th (Service) Battalion, who had first arrived in France at Boulogne on 17 May 1915. The 16th (Reserve) Battalion, remained in England throughout the war, and 1 September 1916, became the 1st Training Reserve Battalion. The 19th (Service) Battalion, 2nd County, was set up by a Parliamentary Recruitment Committee, and became known as a Bantam Battalion. They first arrived in France on 1 February 1916 at Le Havre and before the end of the year 137 of them would be dead.

At the outbreak of the First World War the British Army's minimum regulation height for a soldier was 5ft 3in, but during the war battalions were raised in which minimum height requirement for recruits was reduced to 5ft, enabling otherwise healthy young men to enlist.

The first 'bantam battalions' were recruited in Birkenhead, Cheshire, after Alfred Bigland MP heard of a group of miners who, rejected from every recruiting office, had made their way to the town. One of the miners, rejected on account of his size, offered to fight any man there as proof of his suitability as a soldier, and six men were eventually called upon to remove him. 'Bantam' applicants were men used to physical hard work, and Bigland was so incensed at what he saw as the needless rejection of spirited, healthy men that he petitioned the War Office for permission to establish a fighting unit of undersized men.

The government eventually granted permission, and as news spread across the country, men who had previously been denied the chance to enlist, made their way to Birkenhead, where 3,000 of them were accepted for service into two new 'Bantam battalions' in November 1914. The height requirement had been reduced further, to between 4ft 10in and 5ft 3in.

Although not raised in Durham City, but at nearby Cocken Hall on 10 September 1914, the men of the 18th (Service) Battalion, are worth a mention as they became known as the 'Durham Pals', one of the numerous such battalions which were raised across the country, in an effort to get men to enlist. It was believed that more men would do so if they knew they were going to be serving alongside men from the communities in which they lived and worked. It was a successful tactic but was eventually dispensed with: when these battalions actually went to war, the menfolk of entire communities could be wiped out, in some cases in a single morning.

As the war intensified throughout 1916, so did the casualties. By the end of the year a total of 237,352 Commonwealth soldiers had been killed or died as a direct result of the war. That equates to a staggering 650 men every single day of the year. When it is taken in to account that most large towns didn't even lose half that amount of men throughout the entire duration of the war, the true enormity of that figure becomes apparent. The numbers of men killed in 1916 was an increase of 85,576 on those killed in 1915, which in turn was a daily increase of 234 fatalities.

When trying to make sense of these figures, it becomes clear to see why the Government felt obliged to bring in conscription. They were losing more and more men, but rather than take an in-depth look at some of their tactics and some of the senior officers who were in charge, their favoured way of securing a victory was to force more and more men to enlist, who they could then send to fight.

* * *

Drunkenness was a big issue during the First World War and at one stage the government had real concerns about men spending so much of time drunk that it would seriously affect the war effort on the home front. Ironically, one of the reasons for the increase in drinking was the increase in wages during the war years, as having more money allowed people to drink more.

In 1915, David Lloyd George, had famously said that Britain was 'fighting Germans, Austrians and Drink, and as far as I can see the greatest of these foes is drink.' He took the issue even further in April 1915 when he started a campaign to try and persuade public figures to give up alcohol until the war was over, the assumption being that if an example was set by those in power, then the average man and woman would do likewise. The King himself supported the campaign by announcing that the entire Royal Household would refrain from drinking alcohol until the end of the war. But not everybody was so supportive. The then Prime Minister, Herbert Asquith, who was known as something of a heavy drinker, refused to follow the King's example, which, as can be imagined, caused a certain amount of shock in some sections of society.

One of the measures that was brought in to deal with incidents of drunkenness was to reduce the opening hours of public houses and other licensed premises. Prior to the changes, such premises could open at five o'clock in the morning and stay open the entire day until half past midnight. In cities and industrial areas opening times were reduced to between 12 noon to 2.30 pm, and then again between 6.30 pm to 9.30 pm.

On 19 January 1916, the landlady of the Canteen Inn in Gilesgate, Jane Atkinson, was charged at Durham City Police Court with permitting drunkenness on her premises. The person in question, Christopher Richardson, a miner from the nearby Sherburn Colliery, was charged with being drunk on a licensed premises. Detective Page told the local magistrates that he saw Richardson inside the Canteen Inn at about nine o'clock in the evening on the night in question, and at the time he appeared to have been drunk, as he was staggering all over the place. When Detective Page escorted Richardson to the police station after having placed him under arrest, he was still finding it extremely difficult to walk and kept bumping into people on the way. When he arrived at the police station, Inspector Robson saw nothing in Richardson's demeanour to indicate any alternative suggestion other than that he was drunk. He asked for a doctor and Inspector Robson called for Dr Vann to attend the police station, to whom Richardson admitted to having drunk seven pints of beer.

One of the tests which Dr Vann attempted to have Richardson attempt, was for him to walk along in a straight line with the toe of one foot at the heel of the other. He managed that fairly well. Two other tests Dr Vann used were to have Richardson stand on one leg with both eyes closed, and the other involved a writing test. It is assumed, of course, that Richardson could in fact read and write. After the tests had been completed, Dr Vann concluded that that Richardson's manner was familiar, that his speech was 'thick', possibly what today would be referred to as being slurred. Richardson had no coherence of movement, which led Dr Vann to believe that he was distinctly under the influence of alcohol, but he could not say that he was totally inebriated.

Mr Ferens, who defended Richardson, commented that he felt most men, even in a completely sober state of mind, would have standing on one leg and closing their eyes. Dr Vann disagreed, so as if to prove the point, Mr Ferens tried to do the test himself in court and said: 'Look, I am doing it now and have difficulty in balancing my body, even without closing my eyes.' Intentionally or otherwise Mr Ferens' attempt at debunking the test in such a comical manner provoked laughter from some of those in the courtroom.

Describing Richardson's condition at two o'clock the following morning, whilst in his cell, PC Lund described to the court how he found him stood upon the bench, with his hands in his trouser pockets, whistling and singing away and appearing quite happy. In the circumstances Lund decided just to observe and not interrupt him. In response to this and in an effort to explain his actions, Richardson glibly declared that standing on the bench was the best he could do as it was not a very comfortable bed to lie on. Despite the fact that Richardson had already admitted having drunk seven pints of beer, Mr Ferens informed the court that his client had been waiting for a trap (taxi) and that he had only had two gills of beer (half a pint) in the hour between eight and nine o'clock, and that he was not drunk. Mrs Atkinson, the Pub's landlady, was represented in court by Mr J. Patrick, who contended on her behalf that it would have been impossible for her to have thought Richardson was drunk, and that she believed Richardson to have been quite sober.

The magistrates, having considered all of the evidence put before them, concurred that both of the defendants were guilty as charged and that justice would be best served by ordering them to pay the costs of the court.

* * *

The Military Services Act 1916, which came into force on 27 January, had seen conscription brought in for the first time. It compelled men of a certain age to enlist in the armed forces and go off to fight in the war. All British males were subject of the Act, who on 15 August 1915 were ordinarily resident in Great Britain and who had attained the age of eighteen, but were not yet forty-one years of age, and on 2 November 1915 were unmarried or widowed with dependent children. There were certain automatic categories which made men exempt from having to undertake military training, these included men in Holy Orders or who were a regular minister of any religious denomination.

As is normal in life there is always an 'exception to the rule', Men could make an application before a Military Service Tribunal to acquire a certificate of exemption from having to enlist in His Majesty's armed forces and undergo military training. There were four grounds on which men could make such a claim, these were:

- Where a man was in ill health or infirm.
- Where serious hardship would ensue owing to his exceptional financial or business obligations or domestic position.
- Where it was expedient in the national interests that a man should be engaged in other work, or, if he is being educated or trained for any other work that he should continue.
- Where a man held a conscientious objection to the undertaking of combatant service.

Certificates of exemption could be granted by any Government department to men or classes or bodies of men in their employ, where it appeared to be more convenient for this to take place than by an individual application to a local tribunal.

A certificate of exemption could be issued in three different ways. It could be absolute, conditional or temporary. Where certificates of exemption were issued for continued education or training, or for those issued on the grounds of financial hardship, these could only be temporary. If the conditions under which a certificate of exemption had originally been granted to a man had then subsequently changed, it was his duty to inform the authorities. Failure to do so could result in a prison sentence. Military Service Tribunals up and down the country were quickly inundated with applications by young men who wanted to be exempt from having to undertake military service. Here are just a few examples from a session of Durham Rural District Tribunal which took place on the evening of Tuesday 7 March.

The Agent of the Framwellgate Coal Company applied for the exemption of a man who was both a cashier and an assistant agent, who lived in Durham, on the grounds that he was indispensable, as no adequate substitute could be found, even though there were more than 400 miners working for the company. The Tribunal decided to provide the man concerned with a two-month exemption certificate.

A Durham mining engineer claimed an exemption for his chauffeur, stating that his car was used solely for business purposes in the city, which in the main were in connection with hospital work and not for pleasure. The chauffeur was also somewhat of a dab hand at electrics and dealt with any such related matters at the engineer's home. The claim was disallowed.

A Heyton Lyons assistant schoolteacher applied for postponement to the married groups, on the grounds that he was the only son and sole support of his widowed mother and two sisters. The applicant admitted that his wages would be made up by the County Council if he were to be called up, but stated that it would be a personal loss. He was granted a two-month postponement.

\* \* \*

On Friday, 10 March at the Newcastle Literary and Philosophical Society, a lecture was given by Kenneth H. Vickers, Professor of Modern History at Durham University. His lecture was on the subject of Nationality and Liberalism in relation to International Policy, which with the nation at war, was an interesting if not somewhat intriguing choice of topic.

The original speaker was to have been Mr Richard Oliver Heslop. who was a Newcastle businessman, author, historian, lexicologist, lexicographer, song writer and poet. His most famous work is the second volume of *Northumberland Words*. The 1911 Census showed him as an iron and steel merchant.

Professor Vickers began by making reference to Mr Heslop's sudden and unexpected death on Friday 3 March, and pointing to a chair on the stage next to him and said he thought it better to leave the chair vacant as a symbol of the great void which had been created by Mr Heslop's untimely death.

Professor Vickers' lecture looked at both nationality and liberalism and the problems that were raised by the two ideas, specifically in the period between 1815 and 1830, when they played such an important part in the world of politics. It was a time when a federated Europe wanted a peaceful existence, and war was the last thing on its mind. The main protagonist at the time was France, who had experienced its own social revolution, and its dynamic leader Napoleon Bonaparte, who wanted to conquer and control as much of Europe as he could.

Professor Vickers ended his lecture by saying that a federation of Europe had failed because there were no fundamental agreements between the various countries. How ironic then that the main reason why the First World War drew in so many countries so quickly, was because of the alliances which nations had with their neighbouring countries. Great Britain declared war on Germany, not because of an attack by Germany on her, but because of the latter's invasion of Belgium, a country who Great Britain had an alliance with and was sworn to protect.

\* \* \*

On the evening of Tuesday, 21 March 1916, a special meeting of the Durham City Chamber of Trade took place in the Mayor's Chamber at Durham City Town Hall. The meeting had been called to consider the position of attested married businessmen in relation to the Derby scheme. The Chair of the meeting was Councillor William Smith, who reminded those present at the meeting, that the resolution which they had to consider was:

> That, in view of the undertakings under which men attested, and so long as numbers of unmarried men have not been dealt with,

we strongly urge the Government to consider the personal grievances of the attested married business men, and to make such suitable and proper arrangements as may prevent undue hardships and loss.

Councillor Smith took a pragmatic approach to what was understandably a sensitive subject for some of those at the meeting, asking the members to consider the matter in a common sense, patriotic and level-headed manner. It was however quite straightforward. On the one hand it was about the individual needs and wants of some of the members, balanced against that of the needs of the country. The meeting in part hoped to be able to address and resolve the problem in a satisfactory way, for all parties concerned.

The Derby Scheme was named after Edward Stanley, 17th Earl of Derby, who in the autumn of 1915 became the new Director-General of Recruiting. In essence it was about getting more men to enlist in the Army. Under the scheme Derby required each eligible man aged between eighteen and forty-one who was not in an essential occupation to make a public declaration. When the scheme was announced many men went to the recruiting office and enlisted. Depending on your choice of language, it was either a case of cajoling or embarrassing men to join up, as conscription didn't come in until the beginning of the following year.

There were forty-six separate groups that men were then put into depending on their personal circumstances. They were promised that they would be given fourteen days' advance notice of being called up and that single men's groups would be called upon before the married men's groups, although some single men tried to circumvent this by subsequently getting married. The scheme obtained the signatures of 318,553 medically fit, single men. However, a large percentage of men, both married and single, still publicly refused to enlist. This left the government short of men that it needed to sustain the war. Conscription was introduced early the following year.

Businessmen had been advised that they needed to attest before 11 December, or else they would have no ground for appeal, which was slightly at odds with the overall position, as those who did not attest appeared to be in a better position than those who did. What annoyed some of the members was the attitude of the Tribunals, whose stock response was along the lines of, 'Well, just sell your business', businesses which in some cases had been built up over many years and who employed many other people. Who exactly would they sell them to? In addition they knew that having to sell a business in such circumstances was always going to place them at a disadvantage, as the prospective buyer would more than likely offer a lot less than the business was actually worth.

Mr J.C. Fowler pointed out that they objected to single, unskilled men, looking to work in munitions factories to escape conscription and having to fight, as no married man that he knew wanted to use the excuse of not enlisting, because of having a wife.

Councillor F.W. Goodyear went even further, making his annoyance clear to all those present, when he said that it was a scandal that married men should have to go and fight, whilst a large number of single men were 'hiding' in munitions' factories and earning good wages as well. His submission to the meeting was that the Government should make provision for married men.

At the end of the emotive discussion, Mr Bainton moved that their original motion should be withdrawn and replaced with one that was of the opinion that all tradesmen should be put in to a special reserve for home defence or munitions work, and should be trained within the Parliamentary area in which their business was situated. The motion was seconded by Mr Holiday.

This meeting showed just how strong feelings about the war were by 1916. It had gone on for much longer than had been expected, mainly because of the initial assertions that it would all be over by Christmas of 1914. In the seventeen months from the outbreak of the war up until the end of December 1915, a total of 189,386 men of the Commonwealth forces had been killed and double that amount had been wounded, including 35,500 of whom had been medically discharged from the Army, many with life-changing injuries.

The initial excitement and outpouring of patriotic fervour, national pride and a desire to want to do one's duty had long since dissipated.

\* \* \*

On Friday 24 March a meeting of the Durham City Tribunal took place at the Mayor's Chamber at Durham Town Hall. The Mayor, Councillor J.G. Gradon, presided over the hearing.

Several students from Durham University were claiming exemption on the grounds that they were theological students who had been accepted for ordination, and because they were preparing to sit their final exams. One of the group explained that he was South African and a native of Durban. All of the applications were subsequently withdrawn when it was intimated to the students that it was not within the power of the Tribunal to consider them.

One of the tutors at the same university claimed an exemption on the grounds that he was a conscientious objector, and that he believed that the whole idea of warfare was directly opposed to his Christian principles, and that he was not prepared to undertake any work which was under military control, or was a part of any military organization. He said that he felt there was a good deal of work which needed to be done at home, work which he was more than willing and prepared to perform, as long as it did not bring him under any kind of military authority. The man considered that he was serving his country the best way that he possibly could, by carrying on the work which he was already doing. The Tribunal granted him a conditional exemption.

At the close of the meeting, the Mayor said that the Tribunal had determined that conditional exemptions were suitable and appropriate in the circumstances, but would be surprised if the military authorities did not appeal against these decisions.

\* \* \*

A ceremony took place in Durham City on Tuesday 25 April 1916, when the Mayor, Mr J.G. Gradon, took possession of a captured German field gun from the military authorities, which was to be used for exhibition purposes. The gun had been captured during fighting between British and German forces at Néry, in Oize, northern France on 1 September 1914, during the retreat from Mons.

It was an action which started when a British cavalry unit was attacked by a much larger force of German cavalry. It then progressed into an artillery exchange. By the end of the day, British forces had incurred 135 casualties. So intense was the fighting that three men from 'L' Battery, Royal Horse Artillery, Captain Edward Bradbury, Battery Sergeant-Major George Dorrell and Sergeant David Nelson, were awarded the Victoria Cross.

*Impression of the action at Néry, by an unknown artist.*

The gun had arrived at the city's railway station and was then escorted to the Market Square by detachments from the Royal Army Medical Corps, the Royal Field Artillery as well as the 3rd/8th Battalion, Durham Light Infantry. The band of the 8th Battalion, Durham Light Infantry, under the direction of Bandmaster Henderson, preceded the procession through the streets, which were packed with crowds of people along the entire route. There were plenty of officers in attendance including Lieutenant Colonel J. Burgoyne Johnson, Major W.A. Thompson, Captain Simpson, Adjutant King, Lieutenant and Quartermaster E.M. Grierson, Lieutenant D.E. Ingram, Lieutenant J.H. Burrell, and Lieutenant W.E. Turnbull.

After the procession the Mayor of Durham City invited his colleagues and members of the public to join him in his Chamber to hear the speeches made by some of the invited dignitaries. In handing over the gun, Lieutenant Colonel Johnson remarked that it had been won through the bravery and endurance of the soldiers, probably at the cost of a great many lives and of wounded, and possibly among them were some local men. It was something of a coincidence that it was exactly a year to the day, when the 8th Battalion, Durham Light Infantry had been fighting alongside troops from the Northumberland Division, and though they suffered heavy casualties, they gave a good account of themselves. Major Thompson said that he was pleased on behalf of the local community to receive the gun, and he hoped it would put in their minds a greater determination than ever before to bring the war to a successful termination.

The Dean of Durham also addressed those present, made the somewhat strange statement that the captured gun was like a visitor to the city, and one that they were happy to see, and that they would be happy to see many more similar visitors. The reason behind the gun's arrival and display in the city for a month, was seen by some as being slightly subliminal. Some believed that the longer the gun stayed in the city, the more men would be encouraged to join up to go and fight against the Germans. The gun was interpreted by some as being a symbol of German militarism, and that it was therefore their individual and collective duty to fight against and defeat such evil tyranny.

The Dean of Durham reminded the gathering that the gun was a symbol of a modern war, a war that was being fought by machines as well as men. It was a war that was being fought by the mechanic and the artificer, working in a factory, just as much as it was by the soldier in the trench, and that both citizens and soldiers needed to pull together and work with one another, if the war was to be won. He remarked how some who looked at the German gun stood proudly in the Market Square saw it as a pledge of a coming victory, he said, in a war that had had its highs and lows. The feeling now was a positive one, of expectation of an imminent victory in a matter of months rather than years. Brave British troops would return from the fighting for a final time, their faces no longer shadowed with fear and anxiety, but beaming with a look of triumphant exultation and gratitude for what had been achieved by their efforts, and those of their comrades, some of whom hadn't survived to experience the sweet taste of victory.

Another thought about the gun, he said, was that it reminded some of the price which had been paid for their imminent victory. But that by looking at the gun people were reminded of the 'Faithful Durhams' who had carried in to the fields abroad the name and the fame of England. They thought of them with love and gratitude, in such a way, that they could not find sufficient words to express what they wanted to say.

He waxed lyrical about how the government had sent similar guns to other towns and cities throughout the country, not as a goodwill gesture or because they had a glut of captured German guns that they didn't know what to do with, but because they hoped the arrival of the guns would galvanize support for the troops at the Front, whilst leaving people with a feeling of wellbeing and a stiffening of their resolve, not a trait that he believed the people of Durham required assistance with.

The recruiting officer for the district of Durham, Captain Rogerson, along with Major W.A. Thompson, also addressed the gathering, before the proceedings were concluded by the band of the 8th Battalion, Durham Light Infantry providing a rendition of the National Anthem.

* * *

Another change in 1916 was the introduction of 'Daylight Saving Time' in the Summer Time Act, which meant that between 21 May and 1 October, Greenwich Mean Time plus one hour applied, with the intention of providing more hours in the working day. The idea itself was nothing new and had been around for many years. In principle it was about workers starting work earlier in the summer months so as to make more efficient use of daylight hours. A builder from Farnham in Surrey, William Willets, had picked up on the idea as early as 1907, and had pushed for the idea to become official. The onset of the First World War had finally made the British Government look at the issue more closely, mainly because of the need to save coal supplies, but also to help with boosting much-needed wartime production. Sadly, for William Willets, he did not live to see Daylight Saving Time come into being, as he passed away on 4 March 1915, a victim of influenza. The Summer Time Act came in to law on Wednesday 17 May, and was implemented for the first time four days later on Sunday 21 May. By the time the British Government had acted to bring it in to law, however, Germany had already made the transition.

* * *

By April 1916, more and more women were being employed in agricultural work, thus releasing many men to fight. In April 1916, the Honorary Secretary of the Durham County War Agricultural Committee, William Flemming, wrote a letter to the *Newcastle Journal*. His address was shown as Small Holdings Apartment, 48 Old Elvet, Durham.

> Sir,
> It will be of interest to farmers to know that at a recent meeting of the women's War Agricultural Committee, the reports of the various union representatives, showing the results of the canvas were received. The returns to hand show that 2,935 women have been registered in the county for work on the land, of which, 1,542, had previous experience of such work, and 1,662 are full time workers.
>
> The following are the numbers of workers registered in the different unions; Auckland 194, Barnard Castle 131, Chester-le-Street 577, Darlington 520, Durham 662, Gateshead 159, Hartlepool 55, Houghton-le-spring 179, Lanchester 280, Sedgefield 196, Stockton 129, Weardale 127. The returns are not complete, and a further statement will be available in a short time.
>
> As you are no doubt aware, the committee do not in the least wish to interfere with the farmer and the women workers he usually employs. The efforts of the committee are solely to provide additional women workers to meet the shortage of labour due to enlistment. The committee do not propose to deal with the question of the wages to be paid, but leave this to be settled between the farmer and the worker.

As can been seen this letter, women from Durham City were more than doing their bit for the war effort.

\* \* \*

On Friday, 12 May 1916 the Durham City Military Service Tribunal sat in the Mayor's Chamber at the Town Hall. The Mayor, Councillor Mr J.G. Gradon, Alderman Mr H.E. Ferens, Alderman Mr A. Pattison,

Councillor, Mr P.J. Waite and Councillor Mr G.A. Carpenter, were those hearing the applications for certificate of exemptions. The Clerk was Mr F. Marshall, and the military representative was Major Aubrey White.

The first application of the day was somewhat of a joint affair, and made by five of the city's butchers on behalf of the slaughtermen who were in their employ. After due consideration, a temporary exemption certificate was issued in each of the cases.

An eighteen-year-old student from St Bede's College requested a six-week exemption, so that he could complete his first year's training. The application was granted, in view of the special circumstances in relation to his age.

A grocer's manager applied for a total exemption from having to undertake military service on the grounds of indispensability. Why he was so indispensable was not clear, but remarkably he was given an exemption for six weeks until the end of June. Major White pointed out that such applications could not be renewed time and again, and they could not go on forever.

A master grocer on the North Road applied for exemption, saying he had four girls and two boys in the shop. He had been in the business for eleven years and had put all of his money in to the business. If he had to enlist he had nobody who he could leave in charge to run the business, and would therefore have to close it down. The applicant, who was a single man, was granted an exemption until 31 July 1916.

A father had requested an exemption for his son who was the manager of a carpet factory, on the grounds of indispensability. The business had forty employees of whom twelve were men. The father told the Tribunal that he was the owner of the business, but as he was in failing health he could not run it on his own, especially as since the war had begun, they had become even busier. Major White pointed out that the claimant was already a member of the OTC and was actually in the process of trying to obtain a commission. If successful, his father would certainly have to do without him then, so why could he not do without him now? The claimant stated that joining the OTC was a precaution to get training should the worst come to the worst. Along with another member of staff who was engaged in training women and girls how to weave, an exemption was granted until the end of July.

Two weeks later the Tribunal sat once again in the Mayor's

Chambers, and the same individuals were present to consider the applications, as were the Clerk, Mr Marshall and the Military Representative, Major White. In total the Tribunal had to listen to fifty-one applications, most of whom were granted exemptions for three months: in most of these cases the intimation was made to the applicants that a further appeal could be lodged if they failed to complete business arrangements during the initial period of exemption.

Four university students were granted exemptions until 30 June in order that they might be allowed to sit their forthcoming exams. The Clerk of Durham County Council, Mr Harold Jevons, applied in respect of four officials, three clerks and a road foreman. One of the clerks was engaged in his own office, and he pointed out that of eleven employed immediately under him, at the outbreak of the war, three had enlisted and there were only six remaining. The clerk in question had charge of the papers in connection with the county Appeals Tribunal and other work dealing with the war. All four of the applications were granted exemptions until 31 July.

Mr James Ogg, the Secretary of the Durham County Cokeman's Association, asked for the exemption of his chief and confidential clerk, pointing out that he was the only clerk left. Exemption was granted until 31 August. An application was made by a man who was a travelling draper who said that he had four dependants, his wife and their three children. It was intimated that a two-month period of exemption had been recommended by the advisory committee, so as to give the man sufficient time to wind up his business. The applicant was clearly not happy with such a short period of exemption and said that this wasn't sufficient time as a lot of his business was carried out on credit and suggested that the he be granted an exemption for six months. The Mayor replied that the war might well be over in six months' time! A compromise was reached and the applicant was given a three-month extension until 31 August.

All in all 1916 had seen many changes both on the home front, with new pieces of legislation coming into being, which had affected the civilian population in many different ways, and on the Western Front and in other theatres of war, with the numerous bloody battles that had taken place and claimed so many lives. By now the general feeling amongst civilians and soldiers alike, was for the war and the killing to stop for good.

CHAPTER 4

# 1917
# Seeing It Through

This would be the worst year of the entire war as far as British and Commonwealth casualties were concerned. By the end of the year 294,591 officers and men would be dead, averaging out at 807 for every single day of the year. This was also 57,239 more than had been killed in 1916.

The war had by now reached a point of no return. Having rebutted Germany's proposal to bring the war to an end the previous year, Britain and her allies had no other option but to push on for an outright victory, and to bring the war to an end as quickly as they could, even though they knew that by taking this course of action, thousands more would die.

The year saw many battles and other events. Here are just some of them:

- The Battle of Kut (began 9 January).
- German unrestricted submarine warfare began (1 February).
- The Russian Revolution (began 8 March).
- Tsar Nicholas II abdicated (15 March).
- The First Battle of Gaza (began 26 March).
- United States of America declared war on Germany (6 April).
- The Battle of Arras (began 9 April).
- The Battle of Vimy Ridge (began 9 April).
- The Battles of the Scarpe (began 9 April).

- The Second Battle of the Aisne (began 16 April).
- First Gotha bomber air-raid on London (13 June)
- The Battle of Messines (began 7 June).
- First American troops arrived in France.
- British Royal Family changed its name to Windsor (17 July).
- British Tank Corps formed (28 July).
- The Third Battle of Ypres (began 31 July).
- The Battle of Pilckem Ridge (began 31 July).
- The Battle of Polygon Wood (began 26 September).
- Battle of Poelcappelle (9 October).
- The Battles of Passchendaele (began 12 October).
- Mata Hari executed by French firing squad, for spying for Germany (17 October).
- The Battle of Cambrai (began 20 November).

In January there were 10,503 fatalities, of which 137 were members of the Durham Light Infantry. One of these was Private (27915) Andrew Cranston from the 2nd Battalion, who died of his wounds at 1.45 am on 18 January at No. 33 Casualty Clearing Station, and is buried at the Bethune Town Cemetery in the Pas de Calais, which during the early part of 1917 was an important Allied hospital and railway centre. At the time of his death, Andrew was thirty-two years of age. From looking at the war diaries of the 2nd Battalion, Durham Light Infantry, it is not exactly clear when and where he was wounded, since private soldiers were never individually named in them, only officer casualties.

What the war diaries for the 2nd Battalion, Durham Light Infantry do show is that from 1 to 17 January the battalion was either in the front-line trenches at Cambrin, or being held in reserve at Annequin, having been relieved by the 11th Battalion, Essex Regiment. During all of that time there is no record in the war diaries of the battalion having incurred any casualties. In December 1916 four men were killed, six were wounded and a further three came under the slightly unusual heading of having been 'Accidentally Wounded'. It is more than likely that Andrew was one of the nine men who had been wounded during this month. It could suggest two things: firstly that his wounds were not initially deemed to have been life-threatening, as all badly-wounded men were sent back home to England for further treatment and convalescence, or that he was so badly wounded that he wasn't expected to survive that long. His Army Service Record shows that he was in fact wounded on 17 January, with multiple wounds to the back and forearm, even though there is no mention of any incident in the battalion's war diaries for that day

By the end of the year the Durham Light Infantry had lost a total of 3,051 men. Andrew was a married man, having tied the knot with Harriet Bo Forman in February 1909 in Gateshead. They had three children, a son William and daughters Violet and Margaret, and lived at Rawdon Road, Wallsend-on-Tyne. Before the war Andrew had been employed as a coal miner at one of the local pits.

He had enlisted in the Army on 1 November 1915 at Consett, and as conscription didn't come into force until January 1916, he was most definitely a brave and patriotic volunteer. At the time of his enlistment, his home address was given as 11 Derwent Street, Blackhill, County Durham. After having completed his basic training he arrived in France on 1 June 1916. During his period of basic training at South Shields, his Army Service Record shows that he was officially disciplined on eight separate occasions, mostly for lateness, which cost him a total of thirty-seven days lost pay, by way of punishment. On 15 May 1920, with three children to support, Harriet re-married and in doing so became Mrs Spence, moving in to 103 Kilburn Terrace, Framwellgate, Durham City.

Thomas Chrisp was only twenty-one years of age when the war started, but by the time of his death on 22 June 1917, he had already reached the rank of company sergeant major (300137) and had also been awarded the Military Medal. He served with the 1st/8th Battalion, Durham Light Infantry. He is buried at the Neuville-Vitasse Road Cemetery in the Pas de Calais. It is a small cemetery, with only eighty-six graves from the First World War, Thomas being one of the last two soldiers who were buried there.

Having read the 8th Battalion's war diaries, they show Thomas was actually killed on Saturday, 23 June and not 22 June as is recorded on the entry for him in the Commonwealth War Graves Commission website and on the National Probate Calender and Index of Wills and Administration. He was killed at 8 am, the victim of a German 'Whizz-Bang', which was a generic name given by the British and Commonwealth forces to all German artillery shells, but especially the 77mm. Shells fired by all German light and field artillery travelled at the speed of sound, hence why the 'whizz' sound which was the noise of the shell travelling, before the sound of the bang, which was made by the gun itself. This was a massive disadvantage, as it didn't allow defending troops any time to react. The first they knew about it was when the shell exploded. His late father had been a police inspector at Wooler, whilst before the war Thomas had been a master at St Bede College in the City and had lived with his wife, May Dickinson Chrisp, at Summerleigh, Choppington, in Northumberland. In his Will he left just over £54 to his widow.

Of the three battalions of the Durham Light Infantry that were raised in the City of Durham, during the First World War, the 1st/8th Battalion had forty-nine of its men killed during 1917. The 16th Battalion lost a total of four men killed during the same period, whilst the 19th Battalion lost a total of 156.

Michael Wilson Heaviside was born in Gilesgate, Durham City on 20 October 1880, to John and Ann Heaviside. Together they lived at 4 Station Lane, in Durham City. Eleven years on the family had increased in size and now included daughters, Ethel and Annie as well as another son, Thomas. They were now living at 18 Charles Street, Kimbleworth, Durham and John Heaviside was now employed as a colliery labourer.

When Michael was just seventeen years of age, his mother Annie died on 26 July 1897 aged thirty-seven. It was soon after this that Michael joined the Army. He enlisted as a Private in the Royal Army Medical Corps, and was sent out to South Africa where he served as a stretcher-bearer in the Second Boer War (1899–1902). Once he had completed his period of service with the Colours, Michael was placed on the Army Reserve.

*Michael Wilson Heaviside.*

With the First World War a month old, Michael, by now, thirty-four years of age and working as a miner at the Oswald Pit, Craighead Colliery, was married to Elizabeth. They had three children, sons Richard and John and daughter Annie, named after his mother. Despite the stability of a job, the love of his wife and children, and the fact that he didn't have to enlist, he did the honourable thing and re-joined the Army on 10 September 1914. This time he joined the newly-formed

15th Service Battalion of the Durham Light Infantry, which had been raised in Newcastle. It was part of the 64th Brigade, which was in turn part of the 21st Division.

After having completed his basic training in England he was sent with his regiment out to France. The date he arrived there is not absolutely certain. The British Army Medals Roll index cards for the First World War, record the date he arrived in Boulogne, France, as being on 10 June 1915, whilst other records, including those shown on www.longlongtrail.co.uk, record the date as being 11 September 1915. Once again he served as a stretcher-bearer.

On 8 June, the following citation appeared in the *London Gazette*:

> Victoria Cross for 9710 Private Michael Heaviside, 15th Service Battalion, Durham Light Infantry, *London Gazette* 8 June 1917.
>
> For most conspicuous bravery and devotion to duty. When the Battalion was holding a block in the line, a wounded man was observed about 2 pm in a shell hole about sixty yards away in advance of our block and about forty yards from the enemy line. He was making signals of distress and holding up an empty water bottle. Owing to snipers and machine gun fire it was impossible, during daylight, to send out a stretcher party. But Pte Heaviside volunteered to carry water and food to the wounded man despite the enemy fire. This he succeeded in doing and found the man to be badly wounded and nearly demented with thirst. He had lain out for four days and three nights and the arrival of the water undoubtedly saved his life. Pte Heaviside, who is a stretcher bearer, succeeded the same evening, with the assistance of two comrades in rescuing the wounded man.

*The Victoria Cross.*

On Thursday 12 July Michael Heaviside arrived at his home in Craghead, and received a welcome in keeping with his newfound status as a hero. He was afforded an enthusiastic reception on route from Shield Row railway station to his home in Craghead, passing through Stanley and South Moor on the way. Crowds of well-wishers lined the route to catch sight of the returning hero as well as to congratulate him on his act of bravery and the award of the Victoria Cross.

When he arrived at Shield Row railway station, he was met by members of the Durham Volunteers, the Church Lads' Brigade and the South Moor Colliery Band. The first stop was at the Stanley Council House, where Private Heaviside was officially welcomed by Councillor Patrick Duffy, who was the Chairman of the Urban District Council, and Councillor Daniel Dodd, who was the Vice Chairman. When he finally arrived at Craghead he was met by Mr William Ord, who was the Chairman of the reception committee which also included Mr Henry Greener, the Honorary Secretary of the Committee, Captain Adjutant Saunders from Gateshead, and the Reverend J.B. Eddon, the Vicar of Craghead.

Private Heaviside was at home for just over two weeks before he had to once again leave his wife and children and return to his battalion. During his well-deserved leave, he had to attend numerous functions, as it seemed everybody wanted to congratulate him and wish him well. After all, he was a hero. He had won the highest award it was possible for a British or Commonwealth soldier to receive. What made his achievement even more remarkable, was that he hadn't fired a single shot in anger, nor had he killed an enemy combatant to receive his award, instead, he had helped save the life of one of his comrades.

A presentation took place on Monday, 30 July at Seaham Harbour, when Michael Heaviside returned to his battalion after having received the award of his Victoria Cross from King George V at Buckingham Palace. The proceedings took place on the drill square, and in the presence of the rest of his battalion, who were formed up around the square. Lieutenant Colonel W.H. Briggs of the Durham Light Infantry presented Private Heaviside with a book of War Savings Certificates on behalf of the officers and men of the 15th Battalion, and a cheque for a sum of money which had been collected by the men from his own company. All of the men who belonged to the 15th Battalion were proud of him and wished him good health and a long life so that he could enjoy wearing his decoration for many years to come. He also had the honour of knowing that his name and brave act of heroism would be placed in the annuls of the regiment, alongside others who had performed similar noble and brave acts of heroism whilst in the service of the Durham Light Infantry. When the proceedings were drawn to an end, Private Heaviside was awarded another honour, this time in the form of the men of his battalion marching proudly past him with eyes left. After the war he returned to his family, which by then included eight children, and his job as a miner back in Craghead. He died on 26 April 1939 aged fifty-eight, at his home at Bloemfontein Terrace, Craghead, County Durham. He had been unwell for many years, dating back to the First World War, due to the effects of gas poisoning whilst serving on the Western Front. He is buried at St Thomas's Parish Church in Craghead. Michael's medals, which include his Victoria Cross, were kindly presented by his family to the Durham Light Infantry Museum at Aykley Heads in Durham in July 1957 and are currently on display in the museum's Medal Room.

\* \* \*

On Saturday, 4 August 1917, the third anniversary of the outbreak of war, a meeting took place in the Market Place in Durham, presided over by the Mayor of Durham, Councillor F.W. Goodyear. Also present and in support of the resolution declaring inflexible determination to carry on the war were the county's High Sheriff The Honourable C.A. Liddell, the Dean of Durham Dr H. Henson, Colonel W.C. Blackett TD, Captain The Honourable Adolphus Vane Tempest, Captain J.E. Rogerson, Lieutenant H.E. Ferens, Alderman A. Pattison, Councillor W. Smith, Councillor H.A. Raine, Councillor Edwin Potts, Councillor E.J. Pearce, and the Town Clerk Mr G.A. Carpenter. The Earl of Durham had also been due to attend the meeting, but he was indisposed.

The Mayor began the meeting by making the statement that Germany had placed herself beyond the pale by being the main protagonist for war. He said that Britain owed it to her people and those of other civilized nations, who had no desire or want for war, to ensure that countries such as Germany would never again be in a position to force such a catastrophe onto unwilling nations. He then officially put forward the resolution, which was seconded by the High Sheriff, the Honourable C.A. Lidell, who said, 'All those present wished to beat the Huns, a brutal people who were doing all they could to make life disgusting.'

Dr Henson confirmed his agreement and made comment about America having entered the war on the side of the Allies. He had previously visited the country and spoken with some of their leading figures over the course of the previous three years of the war. He spoke of them as a peace-loving nation who at the start of the war had no desire to become embroiled in a European war which was so far away from their own shores and which ultimately had no direct consequences for herself. The other real consideration for America of course, was because of the large number of Germans living there, might she not consider entering the war on their side, rather than that of Britain and her Allies. Having seen the pain and tragedy which war brought with it, there were those who felt that it should be stopped at all costs, rather than allow it to consume the lives of tens and hundreds of thousands of young men, the longer it continued.

Others saw this kind of peace as being unhealthy, and with it came no guarantees that it would not just start up again sometime in the near future. For the war to end in a constructive manner, Britain and her Allies needed to defeat Germany once and for all. The latter put autocracy over democracy and militarism over liberty, and as long as she held those beliefs, there could be no proper peace. The Allied belief in peace was based on the three R's, Restoration, Restitution and Retribution, and until these elements had been fulfilled, there could be no peace that was worth the sacrifice that Britain had collectively paid as a nation, and the individual sacrifice that her soldiers and their loved ones had also made.

At the same meeting the Mayor honoured some of the City's bravest, with an 'illuminated address' to acknowledge their individual acts of bravery whilst fighting during the war. These awards were paid for out of the Durham City Local Heroes Fund.

- Private (3646) Richard Savage, 10th Royal Hussars. Distinguished Conduct Medal. He had first arrived in France on 6 October 1914. One of Richard's brothers also served during the war, but only for about the first six weeks of his basic training. He was a gunner (51872) in the Royal Garrison Artillery, but was then discharged for being unlikely to make an efficient soldier.
- Corporal (106269) F.G. Cousins, Royal Engineers. Distinguished Conduct Medal. He had enlisted on 15 July 1915 and had then been

medically discharged on 13 August 1917, for no longer being physically fit for war service, because of his wounds.
- Sergeant (11038) W.H. Smith, Durham Light Infantry. Military Medal. He first arrived in France 8 September 1914.
- Private M. Handley, Durham Light Infantry. Military Medal.

\* \* \*

At Durham City Police Court on Monday 27 August 1917, two men stood before the bench, to answer a charge of spitting on the railway's property, namely a carriage of a train.

It was alleged that the men, both labourers, spat on the floor of a train compartment in full view of other passengers, one of whom unfortunately for them, happened to be a police officer, PC Bainbridge, with the National Eastern Railways. On the 5.30 am train from Durham City to Ushaw Moor on 9 August, the two men, both labourers, Joseph Littlefair and John Flowers, were both witnessed spitting on the floor of the carriage by PC Bainbridge. There had been frequent complaints of similar behaviour by labourers by ladies who used the trains and who were horrified at the state of the carriages from spit and phlegm on the floor. Attempts had been made to have the labourers adhere to the warnings that had been given to them about their conduct, but sadly to no avail.

Flowers denied the allegation and Littlefair came out with the feeble excuse in mitigation that he travelled on the trains very little and he couldn't read the warning notice, as if a person didn't understand that spitting on the floor of a train carriage was unacceptable behaviour.

Both men were found guilty and fined five shillings. Flowers who lived at 2 Alma Terrace, Gilesgate, Durham, had seven brothers and one sister.

\* \* \*

A well-known Durham rugby player, Robert Elliot, who was a private (32461) in the 10th Battalion, Loyal North Lancashire Regiment, was killed in action on 11 April. His body was never recovered and his name is commemorated on the Arras Memorial.

Robert's parents Mr Dixon and Mrs Sarah Elliot, who lived at

Gilesgate, Durham City, had finally been given official confirmation of their son's death, four months after he had been killed in action after having been struck on the head by a piece of shrapnel, and was killed instantly. Why there was such a delay in his parents being informed of his death is unclear. He was thirty-six years of age and left behind a widow and a young child. He had been in France since Christmas the previous year.

He was a prominent north-country rugby player, having being a member of the Durham City team that won the cup and he was also in the Durham County side, which won the county championship. He played for his native county against the New Zealand All Blacks touring side. When he retired from playing rugby, he continued in the sport by coaching and training the Gilesgate Junior Rugby Football Club.

* * *

Wednesday, 29 August saw the death at the age of eighty-four of Alderman Ralph Charlton, at his home at Pelaw Terrace in Durham City. Because of his advanced years he was looked upon as the father of the City Council. He was a highly respected and successful local businessman, and one of the most best-known in the community. A dedicated servant of the local community for more than thirty years, Alderman Charlton first arrived in Durham City in about 1877 with two of his brothers-in-laws, Mathias and Robert Stokoe. The three men set up in partnership together in the drapery trade after buying out an already established business in Claypath. The partnership between the three men was later dissolved, but Ralph Charlton continued the business on his own and it went from strength to strength, making him a wealthy man.

He had been involved with the local council since 1888, when he became a member for the St Nicholas area of the City. Four years later in 1892 he was appointed as a Justice of the Peace, and the following year he was appointed Mayor of Durham City, and four years after that he was appointed to the Aldermen's bench.

Outside of his council duties and commitments he was a keen educationalist, serving as one of the City's representatives on the Johnson School Committee, as well as being a manager of the Blue Coates Schools. Politically he was a Unionist and an active member of the Wesleyan Body. He left behind a widow, three daughters and a son who was serving as a lieutenant in the Army.

* * *

On Wednesday, 3 October the sad news was received of the surprise death of a Durham City man, Private (36955) John Vasey of the 21st (Local Reserve) Battalion, Durham Light Infantry. Before the war John had been a butler at Hatfield Hall, in Durham City. In August earlier this year he had been wounded in action whilst serving in France. He was sent back to England to have his wounds treated at Manchester Military Hospital. On the morning of Wednesday 3 October his widowed mother, Mary, received a message from him stating that he would be with her that evening at their home in Union Street, Durham City, to begin ten days' leave before returning to France. At six o'clock that same evening John's family received the tragic and what must have been unbelievable news that John was dead, having been fatally injured on the railway, four miles from Manchester on his way home to Durham. He was thirty-one years of age and well known locally, and had first gone out to France on 2 December 1916 with the 3rd Battalion Durham Light Infantry.

On John's Army Service Record, was a detailed explanation of how he was killed, but it is not sufficiently clear enough to be able to read it. John was in England between 8 December 1915 and 1 December 1916. He arrived in France the very next day and remained there until 29 August 1917, when he was wounded and returned to England on 30 August, where he remained in hospital in Manchester until the day of his death.

On documentation that formed part of his Army Service Record it states that in September 1921, John's widowed mother was living with one of her married daughters, Sarah Bickwell, at 16 Church Street, Durham City. Another married sister, Mary Young, was living at 13 Church Street, Durham City, and another son, William Vasey, was living at Palace Green, Durham City.

* * *

On Friday 12 October, a Military Service Tribunal was held in the Mayor's Chamber at the Town Hall in Durham City, Councillor J.G.

Gradon, presiding. A well-known mineral water-manufacturer, who was also a Durham city councillor, was appealing for an exemption for the driver of his company's lorry. The military representative on the committee, Captain N.W. Apperley MVO, asked the individual, without it having been offered up in mitigation, what success he had made at trying to find a suitable replacement for the driver, in what appeared to be somewhat of a loaded question. The applicant then gave an in-depth explanation as to what lengths he had gone to, to find a suitable replacement. One man he had tried had knocked down a lamp post at Spennymoor, another had knocked one down in Durham City, and another had crashed in to a cart laden with goods. Others who had tried had crashed into a bicycle, one had knocked down a wall at Whitton Gilbert, and there were three occasions where his truck had been driven down embankments by the side of the road. A conditional exemption was granted. It did seem somewhat strange that this particular case hadn't been sent to another Military Service Tribunal so that it could be dealt with fairly and without any undue bias towards the applicant.

* * *

On Wednesday, 7 November a meeting took place of the Durham City Council at the Town Hall. Amongst the matters discussed was a letter that had been received from the 7th Marquis of Londonderry. In it he offered Pelaw Wood to the City as a gift, an offer which not surprisingly was gratefully and readily accepted by the City Council. The Marquis pointed out in his letter that he was selling some of his other properties for the purpose of paying death duties and to meet the heavy burden of taxation which fell upon him. He did not mean his words to be taken as those of complaint, as what he paid in tax he saw as his contribution towards the war effort, and if that helped bring the war to a victorious conclusion, he was more than happy to pay it.

Initially, the Marquis had considered selling off Pelaw Wood, but he changed his mind when he realized how much it meant to the City's people and the pleasure they derived from it in their leisure time. The wood covered a large area of over fifteen acres. The offer had one condition, that the City Council maintained it as a pleasure resort for use by the public for ever more. The wood is situated to the east of

Durham City on the bank of the River Wear, and sits between the districts of Gilesgate and Old Durham. The Marquis's family had a long association with the City, over many generations, with his father having been its Mayor in 1911. He asked that the gift of the wood be associated with the memory of the brave young men from Durham City who had sacrificed their lives in the great cause. The Marquis would be happy in the knowledge that a century later his wishes about the use of the woods, was still been adhered to.

In contrast to this extremely large and generous gift, another was made by His Honour Judge Greenwell, which in its own way was just as valuable, and received with the same amount of appreciation. He presented the Council with a portrait of Count Boruwlaski, which for

*Painting of Jozef Boruwlaski by Philip Reinagle.*

many years had hung in the offices of Messrs Hutchinson and Greenwell in the city. The portrait also came with the violin that the Count was playing as portrayed in the painting.

The Count was in fact a Polish dwarf who was born in 1739 in the city of Halicz (today Halych) in Poland, and who lived to be ninety-seven years of age. His connection with Durham City originates from around the early 1800s, when he accepted an offer from Thomas Ebdon, who was the organist at Durham Cathedral, to live at Banks Cottage in Durham. Boruwlaski made some influential friends in his time in Durham, which included Ebdon, who was a Freemason. It was possibly because of this connection that he was made an honorary member of the Durham Grandby Lodge on 7 October 1806. Boruwlaski died in Durham on 5 September 1837 and was buried in Durham Cathedral.

\* \* \*

Mayoral Sunday in 1917 ironically took place on 11 November. The procession started off from the City's Guildhall and slowly made its way to Durham Cathedral. There were large contingents from the Durham City Boy Scouts, the Durham City Church Lads' Brigade, who were led by the Reverend T.P. Tindall, the curate of St Nicholas Church, as well as the Durham School's OTC, who were proudly led by the school's headmaster, The Reverend R.D. Budworth.

The streets between the Guildhall and the Cathedral were lined with crowds of enthusiastic spectators and it was commented on as to how smart the boys of both the Scouts and the Lads' Brigade were turned out. The whole procession was led by a bugle band who played keenly along the route.

The young men from the OTC were also well turned-out, as would be expected of men of their standing and aspirations. They had all greatly benefitted from their military training, which they had been provided with by an instructor from the regular army.

The next Mayoral Sunday, which was always the first Sunday after the start of Mayor's year of office, which began on 9 November was destined to be a grand affair.

\* \* \*

The poor standard of housing was an issue in Durham City and had been for some time. Many had spoken out on the issue, none more prominent that the Dean of Durham, Dr H. Hensley Henson. The date of his sermon was prophetic given it was made on 11 November, and it came from no more prominent place than the pulpit of Durham Cathedral.

In his sermon he spoke of the unsatisfactory state of affairs in relation to housing, but once again the question was who was responsible, who was to be held to account, for the poor and overcrowded housing situation in the city: 'There were many persons living in Durham under conditions which could not be defended, and ought not to be tolerated one day longer than was absolutely necessary.' One of the difficulties of the time was a transient workforce, mainly low paid, unskilled labourers who had no real option but to move to where the work was available at any given time, or better described as the 'tides of economic movement'. The Dean continued.

> It is certainly arguable that if permanent and adequate housing is to be provided for these people, the responsibility belongs rather with the mine owners who employ them rather than the city of Durham; and that any equitable solution of the problem of housing must give fair application to the principle that the suitable housing of the men employed should be a first charge on the mining industry. Confessedly then, the question of housing in Durham is neither simple in itself nor easy to answer wisely.

Perhaps looking at the issue purely from a religious perspective, the Dean suggested that the city did hold some of the responsibility for providing housing for part-time members of their community. 'We ought to be willing, even at some sacrifice to ourselves, to co-operate with the central authority of the state in finding an answer, which shall remove at last what is the darkest shadow on the public credit of our ancient and beautiful city.'

The Anglican Church at that time was an extremely powerful institution. Nearly everybody went to church on a Sunday morning, as it played such an integral part of everyday life. People were often christened, married and buried at the same parish church. The chances are that their own children had also been christened and married there as well. What the political viewpoint on the issue was, as far as Durham City Council were concerned, or what they felt about the Dean's sermon, is not known.

Ten days earlier the Dean had made a speech at the quarterly meeting of the South Shields Public Health Society on the same subject. It was entitled, 'Housing as the first step in Social Reconstruction.' The meeting drew in a large audience, including the Mayor of South Shields, Alderman W. Allon, as well as other local dignitaries. The Dean spoke of the war and the massive sacrifice which had been made by so many. A war that was unprecedented in its scale, the like of which had never been seen before. If the horrors, pain and suffering of the previous three years, were to have any lasting relevance, then it had to be justifiable in the conscience of everybody, whether they be soldier, wife or mother. This justification could come, so the Dean suggested, in the form of better and improved housing which was a universal need, and not just one that Great Britain needed to address. The sacrifice that had been made by so many could not be allowed to be all in vain, better housing was one way of making sure that the need for the war had counted for something in the long term.

The reason why the Dean saw housing and reconstruction as being so important, was because as far as he was concerned, it was the start of the cycle of humanity. The limited supply of housing was restricting the number of families, which in turn meant fewer children being born, which was never good for the long-term aspirations of a country. This was a time where people didn't live with each other outside of wedlock, that was just not socially acceptable, and to have a child in those circumstances was even worst, especially for the child, who then had to contend with the stigma on their birth certificate of being labelled a bastard.

\* \* \*

The year ended on a high note in Durham City, with the festive celebrations sitting side by side with bittersweet memories of loved ones lost, but not forgotten.

On Christmas Day patients in the Durham County Hospital were cheered by the Christmas fare that was provided and the kind gifts of other edible items. The wards had been nicely decorated by the matron, staff and friends of the hospital to help add to the festive atmosphere. Inmates of the Durham City Workhouse were also looked after and provided with a Christmas they could have least expected, but one that they would have certainly remembered.

Wounded and injured soldiers, who were convalescing at the Durham Voluntary Aid Detachment Hospital, were well catered for in the Bailey, with both food and presents being provided for one and all. The City's poor children were provided with a Christmas breakfast that was paid for by Alderman Samuel Galbraith, who was the representative for the area of Mid-Durham, and which took place in the pleasant surroundings of the Shakespeare Hall.

All in all, not a bad end to the year as 1917 drew to a close, and less than eleven months before the war would be finally over.

CHAPTER 5

# 1918
# The Final Push

Twenty-six major battles took place in 1918, in what would turn out to be the final year of the war. A massive total of 268,185 British and Commonwealth soldiers were killed in the final eleven months of the war, which averages out at a staggering 796 men for each and every one of those days.

With the continuation of such heavy losses, and with no immediate or obvious end in sight, it was quite remarkable just how motivated and committed British soldiers remained in carrying out their duty. Very few, if any, would have had any idea of the overall picture of the war, and how the final outcome would be affected. For most, all they would have known about were the German soldiers in the trenches a matter of a few hundred yards away from their own positions, where they would have to remain for days at a time. That's as far as their world existed.

It was nearly three months in to the year before one of these major battles was fought, when the Second Battle of the Somme took place between 21 March and 5 April, but it was to also be the first of two battles of the Somme, which took place that year, with the third between 21 August to 3 September. It was actually a German military operation which was the start of their Spring Offensive. Their idea was for to break through the Allied lines near Saint-Quentin, then push on towards the Channel ports. If they could gain control of them, they would then be able to stop supplies getting through to the British and

Allied forces, which in turn would leave them with no other option but to retreat back towards the Channel. Just two days into the offensive, the German commander, General Erich Ludendorff, changed his plans and had his armies push westwards in an attempt to split the British and French Armies in the middle, but the plan didn't work, and the Germans were finally defeated at Villers-Bretonneux. Why Ludendorff suddenly and so dramatically changed his plans, isn't known.

The last battle of the war which began on 4 November, just a week before hostilities finally came to an end, was the Battle of the Sambre, which also included the Battle of Thierache and the Second Battle of Guise. British forces were looking to cross the Sambre-Oise Canal at one of the thirty-eight along the canal's 71km length. The problem with this was that each of the locks were heavily defended by German machine-gun teams and infantry. To combat this threat the British decided to put in place a series of small footbridges to allow their men to get across the canal as safely as they could in the circumstances. The main British units involved that day were the 2nd Battalion, Royal Sussex Regiment, the 2nd Battalion, Manchester's and elements of the Lancashire Fusiliers.

A total of 2,765 British and Commonwealth soldiers were killed or died on 4 November, albeit not all of them in the Battle of the Sambre. The Royal Sussex had sixty of its men killed that day. The Manchester Regiment had sixty-seven men killed and the Lancashire Fusiliers lost eighty-two. These figures do not of course include any casualties who were wounded, only those who were killed.

Meanwhile back in the City of Durham, life was continuing as normal as it possibly could do in the circumstances. One of the first major events took place on 11 January, with the news that Durham City Council had decided to bestow upon Dr Herbert Hensley, the Dean of Durham and the Bishop-Designate of Hereford, the honorary award of the Freedom of the City. They also decided to do the same for the Reverend Henry Gee, Master of Durham University, Chaplain-in-Ordinary to the King and Chaplain to the Durham Corporation, who had also recently been appointed as the Dean of Gloucester.

Previous recipients of this honour included the late Alderman W. Boyd, who was the Mayor of Durham on four separate occasions, the late Alderman James Fowler, who was the Mayor of Durham on five occasions, Sir Hedworth Lambton, the brother of Lord Durham, the late Earl Roberts, Matthew Fowler, who was an Alderman of the City as well as its MP, the Earl of Durham KG, and the late Marquis of Londonderry KG.

The new recipients of the award had some very well-known local individuals to compare themselves with, by being in receipt of such an historic honour. It was certainly not an award that was given out lightly, and certainly not one that was ever given to a working-class man, remembering of course that First World War Great Britain was still a very class-ridden society.

Several hundred schoolchildren from the City of Durham, in company with their friends and relatives, attended a carol service at Durham Cathedral to help celebrate, Holy Innocents' Day which is a Christian festival which commemorates the massacre of the innocents in Herod's time when he dictated that all infants under the age of two should be killed. The Mayor of Durham, the Dean of Durham, Dr H. Hensley Henson, other Cathedral clergy, as well as those from around the district, attended. The usual array of Christmas carols were sung both with passion and vigour by both the choir and the congregation. The Reverend H.S. Dennett, delivered an address to those present. His speech was very well delivered and favourably received and was a very inspiring one, just what was needed at such a time.

\* \* \*

On 1 February 1917 Germany had resumed unrestricted submarine warfare, which meant the sinking of any and all shipping, without warning, by their U-boats in and around British waters and in the Mediterranean. The effect, although not immediate, was soon felt, as Great Britain relied heavily on imported food to feed its population.

By the beginning of 1918 it was fair to say that because of the havoc wreaked by the German U-Boats, Britain was struggling to cope with the losses of the much needed food that had failed to reach her shores. By the end of the war Germany had sunk nearly 5,000 Allied and neutral ships, which averages out at about 95 ships for every month of the war, or one ship sunk every three days, which is truly staggering. The shaded areas on the following map, shows the unrestricted submarine warfare zone as was announced by Germany on 1 February 1917. With most of the supplies which Britain needed being sent across

*Shaded areas show the unrestricted submarine warfare zone. (Wikipedia)*

the Atlantic Ocean from ports along the east coast of America, the German Navy knew only too well where she had to focus her U-boats' attacks.

With the Atlantic being the second biggest ocean in the world and prior knowledge of the routes the ships would be taking to reach their final destination, they certainly had plenty of time and space to plan their attacks.

The German campaign began quite successfully, and by April, a month in which 860,000 tons of shipping was lost to the U-boats, Great Britain was down to just six weeks' wheat reserves. The effects on Great Britain's civilian population were not immediate, but by July 1918, the authorities were left with no other option but to bring in rationing for butter, margarine, lard, meat and sugar. Some local authorities had brought it their own localized rationing system months earlier.

In February 1918, the Advisory Committee of the Durham City, Brandon and Byshottles Urban and Durham Rural District, had decided upon a scheme of rationing. After receiving approval from the District Commissioner, the scheme was in place by the end of March. It was based upon the issuing of individual tickets and not on a household system, and to in ensure that nobody was missed out of the scheme, a new register was taken of all addresses and the numbers of people who lived in them.

Application forms were delivered to each and every household throughout Durham City, with the householder having the responsibility of providing the required information and the personal details of everybody living in each dwelling. Tickets were then issued to each individual for the purchase of tea (no coffee), butter, margarine, bacon, cheese and meat. There were separate tickets for each food item, and all householders had to register themselves and their families with local retailers. It was not a requirement of the scheme to register with only one shop for all of the items, but once registered with a particular retailer, individuals could not then subsequently re-register somewhere else.

In order to meet the requirements of disabled people, who in 1918 were referred to as invalids, a special ticket system was introduced. This also applied to individuals who undertook heavy manual labour, as well as travellers and music-hall artistes. For all individuals who came in to this category, their tickets included the name of the shop where they were to obtain their food from. Such tickets could only be obtained from the Executive Officer of the Durham City Advisory Committee.

A month earlier, the Egg Restriction Order 1918 came into force on 25 February, which prohibited the use of eggs in any form for purposes other than human consumption, except under a special licence granted by the Food Controller. However, the use of eggs for breeding chickens was specially exempted from the provisions of the order.

\* \* \*

A meeting of the Durham County War Agricultural Committee took place at the Shire Hall in Durham on Thursday 25 April 1918, Sir Frank Brown presiding.

With Britain feeling the full effects of unrestricted submarine warfare, there was a big drive throughout the country to grow more food, and the county of Durham had been tasked with finding 25,000 acres of land for cultivation, which they had done.

The ready supply of soldiers to carry out this extra farm work had been well maintained, and the reports of the time suggest that their work was 'fairly satisfactory'. Arrangements had also been made to utilise the labour of skilled German prisoners of war, as well as training up women to do the work as well.

There was also a big push across the entire county of Durham to increase the allotment spaces available, so that more and more people could grow their own fruit and vegetables.

\* \* \*

On Saturday, 6 April an educational conference took place at the Durham Miners' Hall, the idea of the Central Labour College. A resolution was submitted at the conference, by those running it, the North of England Branch of the Central Labour College, which had its headquarters in London. The idea was to provide independent education for working-class people, which would be provided by the Central Labour College. This was yet another example of changes in society as the war slowly proceeded towards its conclusion. People already wanted and expected more out of life. A terrible price had been collectively paid by all those concerned, and the working classes in particular were not willing or prepared to return to the social conditions which had been in place before the outbreak of the war. One of the doors to a better way of life was undoubtedly education, which in the main had been for those from the upper classes. Colleges and universities were establishments that were very expensive, and those from the working classes could ill afford such luxuries.

The objective of the conference was to establish six colleges in different parts of the country, one of which would be situated in the north-east of England. The education which would be provided would be suitable and relevant to the working classes. It would be something that could be used as a positive instrument in their hands, rather than a burdensome weight hanging round their necks. A good education such as this scheme provided, would hopefully allow the working-class man to achieve his emancipation, whilst helping to prevent further wars, and dismantle the extremes of the class system, such as wealth and poverty.

After a lengthy and lively discussion, the resolution was passed by the ninety-four delegates who were present from co-operative societies, trade union branches and branches of the Independent Labour Party.

\* \* \*

In May 1918, Alderman John T. and Mrs Mary I. Boyd, of Byland Lodge, Durham, placed a memorial tablet in St Nicholas Parish Church in Durham, in memory of their late son, William, who had been killed in action on 5 November 1916, during the last weeks of the Battle of the Somme.

At the time of his death he was twenty-two years of age and a lieutenant serving with the 8th Battalion, Durham Light Infantry, which was a Territorial unit. Most of its recruits came from Durham City and its surrounding areas. The battalion, on being mobilized in August 1914, were in camp in fields immediately outside of Ravensworth Castle, near Gateshead, to begin their preparations for war. They first arrived in France on 17 April 1915, but the British Army Medal Rolls Index Cards show William as not having arrived there until 6 May 1915.

The Boyds had another son, Fred, as well as five daughters. By the time Williams three campaign medals were sent to his father on 8 June 1923, the family had moved to 51 Clay Path, Durham. To make their loss even more hard to take, William's body was never recovered, and his name is commemorated on the Thiepval Memorial.

There is a photograph, which is held at the Durham County Record Office, of a group of six officers of the 8th Battalion, Durham Light Infantry, which was taken in Cassel in France in April 1915. The six officers are Lieutenant Colonel J. Turnbull, Captain, J. Turnbull, Lieutenant E.A. Leybourne, Lieutenant P. Kirkup, Lieutenant F.M. Weeks and Lieutenant C.L.B. Whall. Remarkably, all six men survived the war. (As an aside, there were twenty-six men with the surname Turnbull who were killed whilst serving with the Durham Light Infantry during the First World War.)

\* \* \*

An article appeared in the edition of the *Newcastle Journal* dated Saturday 22 June. It concerned a Captain and Adjutant J.H. Burrell, of the Durham Light Infantry, whose parents, John and Mary Burrell, had officially been informed that their son had been reported as 'missing' on 27 May. On this day the 1st/8th Battalion of the Durham Light Infantry had thirty-eight officers and men killed in action during the fighting of the Battle of the Aisne. Sadly, only the bodies of ten of these men were recovered. Those whose bodies were never found have been commemorated on the Soissons Memorial, in the Aisne region of France.

Burrell was educated at the Durham School where it was noted that he was quite gifted at playing cricket, rugby and football. On leaving there, he went on to become a student at St John's College, Cambridge, where he received a BA. Whilst at Cambridge, he also joined the OTC and when he enlisted in the Army, he did so as a Sergeant Instructor. He later obtained a commission with the Durham Light Infantry, and served with them in France, arriving there on 5 September 1916.

As best as I can make out this refers to John Hugh Burrell, who was a captain in the 1st/8th Battalion, Durham Light Infantry, and in 1911 he was a boarder at the Durham School. Some other pupils who were boarders at the school at that time, and who also went on to serve in the war, were:

*The Soissons Memorial. (Commonwealth War Graves Commission)*

- John Theodore Gordon **Humphreys** was a lieutenant in the 40th Pathan Indian Infantry. He was gazetted as a lieutenant on 26 May 1917 and was killed in action two months later on 19 July, aged twenty-one, at the Battle of Mgergeri in East Africa, when he was killed by a machine-gun burst whilst leading his men in an effort to assist his commanding officer. His colonel wrote of him; 'He was considered a brave officer and a good comrade, and that was the best that could be said of a soldier.' Another of his senior officers, Captain Wadeson, wrote: 'Your son was regarded in the Regiment as a brave and promising officer, and his loss is keenly felt by all. He was always cheery and willing, however trying the circumstances, and did very good work in the action at Rombo, on 18 April last, when Major Macpherson was killed. On that operation he moved about coolly under heavy fire.' He is buried at the Dar Es Salaam War Cemetery in Tanzania.
- Philip Herbert **Douthwaite** served as a private (376516) with the 18th Battalion, Durham Light Infantry, having enlisted on 12 July 1916 in Oxford where he was an undergraduate at the city's

university, first arriving in France on 16 June 1917. He survived the war and was demobilized on 1 January 1919.
- Reginald Claude Moline **Gee**, MC, was an acting captain with the 15th Battalion, Durham Light Infantry, when he was killed in action on 7 November, four days before the signing of the Armistice.
- Cyril Lancelot Thorald **Barclay** rose to the rank of captain in the Labour Corps, having first arrived in France on 11 May 1917. He survived the war.
- Loftus Gwen Leslie **Peacocke** was a lieutenant in the 1st Dragoon Guards, but didn't join the Army until 1920, going on to serve until 1935. He was awarded the General Service Medal for service in Iraq on 22 December 1923.

Burrell also survived the war, having been captured. Just part of the story of pupils of the Class of 1911 at the Durham School.

\* \* \*

In August the state of housing in Durham City was in the news after a women and her child had died in the property which they had been living in. At the subsequent inquest the Coroner, Mr Graham, had described the property as, 'one of the rookeries [i.e. slums] of the city'. As a result of his comments an inspection of the property had been carried out by the Chairman of the Health Committee, but the house had been found to be in very good order, and was far from being a 'rookery' as the Coroner claimed. The house in question, and other similar properties nearby, had been inspected and were all in at least fairly good condition. Despite this the Chairman of the Health Committee did add that he felt it was still incumbent on the occupants of these properties not only to keep themselves clean, but to do the same for their houses as well. He also pointed out that many of the tenants of these properties worked at many of the district's collieries, and that if the owners of these premises provided more accommodation for their workforce, this would greatly relieve the city's overcrowding problems.

\* \* \*

On Monday 19 August the Durham Miners Association held a meeting to discuss proposals for having women working at the pit head, so that more men can be used for work underground. There was a lengthy and at times somewhat heated discussion and at the end of the meeting, which included representatives from all round the county, there was a near-unanimous decision not to employ women to work at the pit head. The Executive Committee of the Durham Miners' Association suggested that the miners should be prepared to work on Saturdays, and that an effort should be made to reduce the amount of absenteeism amongst the men, but both of these were rejected.

Men who were genuinely sick or who were off due to a work-related accident, had a genuine reason for not being at their place of employment, but it was those who simply didn't turn up because they couldn't be bothered to or because they had a hangover from the night before, that were the ones who needed sorting out. Because of them, the men who were at work, had to work harder which meant they would tire more quickly, which in turn made the likelihood of an accident occurring greater. This raises the question why men would then vote against the suggestion of trying to sort this very issue out, when ultimately it was for their benefit and safety.

* * *

In September 1918, despite the war still not being over, the outcome by no means guaranteed, men still dying at the Front, and food being in short supply, there were some men who still believed it was acceptable to go out on strike for more money. Easy as it is for me to comment a century later, and without being in possession of all of the facts, it still doesn't feel that it was the right thing to do.

The strike was by Durham Corporation workers who wanted an additional war bonus of eight shillings. The men were prepared to return to work if the Corporation agreed to submit their claim to arbitration, something which they had refused to do right from the very beginning of the strike action. So strong was the feeling about the matter that a meeting had been held in Durham City marketplace, and presided over by Mr T.H. Cann, who was the Secretary of the Durham Miners. Others who addressed the meeting were Mr W.P. Richardson, Mr Will Sherwood, who was the Labour candidate for neighbouring

Hartlepool, and Mr Parker McMann, the District President of the striking workers' union. At the end of the meeting it was agreed that the Corporation would be contacted and asked to receive a deputation of union officials. A similar request had previously been refused.

Strikes seem to be a theme running through September 1918 in Durham. Mass meetings took place in six different locations across the county on Saturday, 14 September, when resolutions were carried demanding an eight-hour working day, for all workers who did not already have that luxury, the abolition of the minimum wage rules, and of the 1879 basis, the amendment of the present Conciliation Board, and the substitution of a more equitable system, and expressing the opinion that a substantial increase of the national output of coal could only be secured by the Government returning experienced miners who were in the Army to the pits at once.

At the meeting that was held in Durham City, Mr T. Neville, remarked that the colliery management could have done more in the matter of increasing the output of coal, and much more could have been done if the men had given of their best. He realized and accepted that a fair allowance should have been made for men who were either sick or who had been injured as a result of accidents, but that those who were habitually off sick one or two days a week, even though they were physically fit, needed to get themselves back to work, so that they could help produce the amount of coal that was needed by the 'lads' fighting at the Front.

On the same day another meeting took place at the Marsden Miners Hall at Imeary Street in South Shields. One of those present, Mr Thomas Trotter from Durham, stated that on the issue of wages, the owners of the collieries should come clean about how much it cost to produce the coal as well as how much it was sold for, so that they might be able to form an idea of the profit that was being made, so that the workers might receive a fair share of the profits.

\* \* \*

Charles Young Adamson's story actually begins in Durham, where he was born, and attended the Durham School, but also includes America and Australia. His father, John Adamson, who was a 'beer seller' by trade, was born in Wisconsin in America. Charles was a keen and proficient sportsman at both rugby union and cricket. In 1899, he travelled to Australia with the British Lions Rugby team on their first official touring team, where he played in all four test matches, having never represented the England national team.

After the tour he remained in Australia where he played cricket for the Valley District Cricket Club in Brisbane. Back in England he had previously played cricket for Durham in the Minor Counties Championship. Charles brother-in-law, Lewis Vaughan Lodge, had played international football for England, earning five Caps. He had also played First Class cricket for Hampshire.

Soon after this, he first enlisted in the Australian military, joining the 4th Queensland Imperial Bushmen as Private 273. They left for South Africa from Brisbane aboard the *Port of Manchester* on 18 May 1900, to take part in the Second Boer War. The 4th were in involved in heavy fighting throughout most of August, September, October and November of 1900. They lost four men killed and another four wounded, one of whom, Lieutenant J. Higson, later died of his wounds. The officers and men of the 4th Queensland Imperial Bushmen sailed for home on 7 July 1901, although Adamson signed off in South Africa and made his way back to Durham. He was a stockbroker before the First World War, and with his wife Katherine, and their two sons, Charles and John, they lived at 28 Nevilledale in Durham. Because of Charles's work the family were affluent enough to be able to afford to employ a servant.

By the outbreak of the war, Charles, was already thirty-eight years of age. At the time of his death on 17 September 1918, when he was killed in action, he was a captain and quartermaster with the 8th Battalion, Royal Scots Fusiliers. He is buried at the Karasouli Military Cemetery, which is situated near the town of Polykastro (formerly Karasouli), in Greece. In his will, which was read on 29 January 1919 in Durham, Charles left the sum of £1,153, which it would appear was left to James William Lodge, a solicitor and Matthew Fowler, who was an auctioneer.

These were just a few of the many stories which help give a clear picture of what day-to-day life was like for people back home in Durham City. The combination of the emotional and mental aspects of dealing with the war were not easy for anybody. But no matter what the personal loss was, people had to deal it, and try to get on with their everyday lives as best they could.

CHAPTER 6

# Voluntary Aid Detachments

Medical treatment for soldiers wounded in battle had never been that high on the agenda of marauding armies over the years. The best that a wounded combatant could hope for was either a hot iron to cauterize an open wound or the sawing off of a limb in an attempt to prevent gangrene and a slow, painful death.

The Crimean War lasted from October 1853 to February 1856, and was fought between the Russian Empire and a coalition consisting of the Ottoman Empire, France, Sardinia and Great Britain. During the two and a half years of the war, Great Britain lost a total of 21,097 men, which in relation to the First World War was a comparatively small number. However, what is really staggering is the breakdown of that figure. A total of 2,755 were killed in action and another 2,019 subsequently died of their wounds, whilst a staggering 16,323 died of disease.

The Crimean War is also remembered for the nursing skills, care and compassion shown by Florence Nightingale and her nurses, towards wounded British troops. Nightingale, her thirty-eight volunteer nurses and fifteen Catholic nuns, arrived at Selimiye Barracks in Istanbul, in early November 1854. What they found on their arrival must have come as a shock. There were simply not enough medical staff to look after the large number of wounded soldiers. Added to this, hygiene was poor and food was in short supply, as were much needed medicines, and there appeared to be something of an attitude of indifference towards wounded soldiers, sadly viewed as a hindrance by officialdom.

It is clear that it was Florence Nightingale who laid the foundations

*Cornet Assistant Surgeon Henry Wilkin, 11th Hussars.*

of professional nursing with the opening of her nursing school, the first of its kind, not just in Great Britain but the world, at the prestigious St Thomas' Hospital in London, on 9 July 1860. A group of between twenty to thirty trainees spent a year studying to become qualified nurses.

Thankfully, because of the continuation of the work around nursing that had been started by Florence Nightingale, by the outbreak of the First World War the British and Commonwealth countries were as well prepared as they could possibly be, in a medical sense.

In 1909, still five years away from the outbreak of the First World War, the War Office issued the Scheme for the Organization of Voluntary Aid to assist the Territorial Forces Medical Service, in the eventuality of the nation becoming embroiled in a war. By 1910 there were more than 6,000 volunteers, all of whom were trained in first aid and nursing skills.

*A posed photograph of Florence Nightingale, circa 1860. (Unknown photographer)*

The number of volunteers continued to grow, especially when coupled with the similarly officially recognized volunteers from the Order of St John of Jerusalem, better known today as the St John Ambulance Brigade. The two bodies united to form the Joint War Committee, to ensure that their wartime efforts were being run efficiently and effectively. In the main, Voluntary Aid Detachment (VAD) nurses worked in hospitals and convalescent homes, performing general nursing duties, administering basic first aid, carrying out administrative work and working in the kitchens.

In the County of Durham, there were a grand total of twenty-seven VAD hospitals, but there were only two in Durham City. One was at 17 North Bailey, which was known as the 5th Durham VAD Hospital. The building still exists and today as part of St Chad's College at the University of Durham. The other was at Brancepeth Castle, which is five miles south west of the City of Durham, and was the 7th Durham VAD Hospital. Today it is a private residence.

## 5th VAD Hospital, 17 North Bailey, Durham

It was harder to locate the women and men who had worked at the 5th VAD Hospital, but here are just a few of those who worked at 17 North Bailey in Durham.

Miss Ellen **Brown**, lived at 29 Western Hill, Durham, and served as a Ward Orderly between 4 November 1918 and 29 May 1919. She originally worked at the USA Hospital at Tottenham St Annes, before transferring to the Canadian Hospital at Buxton in Derbyshire, on 12 December 1918.

Miss Marjory **Gradon**, lived at Lynton House, Durham. Her service with the VAD commenced on 1 May 1915. Her main duties were cooking and nursing, and she was classed as occasional staff, working on 310 days of the year.

Cissie Otto **Lilly** certainly did her bit during the war. Her home was in Tynemouth on the north-east coast in Tyne and Wear. Before becoming part of the staff of the 5th Durham VAD, she had previously worked for the 2nd Durham VAD at South Shields and the Jubilee Infirmary at North Shields, as well as the 5th Northumberland VAD Hospital. She first enrolled on 17 January 1915 as a Grade 2 nurse and served for the rest of the war. Her service number was L/457 and on 9 May 1919 she was awarded her Class 2 Scarlet Efficiency medal.

Mrs Dorothy S.R. **Moore**, lived at The Vicarage in South Hetton, and served as a VAD nurse between 1 October 1915 and 31 July 1917. Her main duties were to provide massage treatment for those convalescing soldiers who required it because of their injuries. She was occasional staff, working for just six hours a week.

John Ernest **Smith**, lived at 24 High Street, Lamgley Moor, Durham City. His service number was 9647 and he worked as an orderly, but his service record sadly did not record which VAD hospital he was employed at.

## 7th Durham VAD Hospital, Brancepeth Castle

Miss Emily **Argument** lived at The Tilery, Willington, County Durham, and worked as a nurse at Brancepeth Castle, Durham. She began working there on 21 July 1915 and remained there until 12 October 1916.

Miss Norah **Austin** lived at The Willows in Sunderland, but worked

*Brancepeth Castle. (Photograph by Oliver Dixon)*

at Brancepeth Castle as a trained nurse between 18 March 1916 and 31 December 1917. She was paid twenty-one shillings a week.

Miss Mary **Best** lived and worked at Brancepeth Castle. She worked there between 1 January 1917 and 28 February 1919, as a part-time kitchen maid and private servant.

Miss Mary **Bowes** lived at 65 Sunderland Street, Brandon, County Durham and worked as a nurse at Barncepeth Castle, between 6 May 1918 and 28 February 1919.

Vicountess Margaret Selina **Boyne**, CBE, was by all accounts quite a character. She was the benefactor who allowed Brancepeth Castle to be used as a hospital during the war. She was also the most distinguished member of staff ever to work for the 7th Durham VAD. During the war her home address was 'Hardwick' in Sedgefield. Her rank was that of an officer and she was engaged on general nursing duties between 3 December 1914 and 15 March 1919.

Bertha **Bradish** lived and worked at Brancepeth Castle and was employed as a part-time kitchen maid and a private servant between 3 December 1914 and 28 February 1919.

Miss Ellen **Brothers** lived at Quarry Hill, Brancepeth and worked at Brancepeth Castle between 10 March 1916 and 21 June 1917 as a nurse.

Miss Jean **Brotherstow** lived and worked at Brancepeth Castle between 1 June 1915 and 28 February 1919 as a pantry maid and private servant.

Miss Alice **Bushell** lived at Quarry Hill, Brancepeth and worked at Brancepeth Castle, between 19 December 1915 and 5 May 1918 as a nurse.

Miss Anne **Butcher** lived and worked at Brancepeth Castle as a cook and a private servant, between 1 May 1915 and 28 February 1919.

Mrs Elizabeth **Calvert** lived at Willington House, Willington, County Durham, and worked as a nurse at Brancepeth Castle. She began working as a VAD on 10 June 1916 and remained until 31 July 1918.

Miss Norma **Chapman** lived at Rough Lea Terrace, Hornwich, Willington. She worked at Brancepeth Castle between 10 November 18 as a nurse.

Miss Alice Mary **Coates** lived at Clyde House and worked at Brancepeth Castle between 7 February 1918 and 21 February 1919, as a part-time nurse.

Mrs Cecil **Crawley** lived at Quarry Hill, Brancepeth and worked at Brancepeth Castle between 10 May 1915 and 2 November 1918 as a part-time nurse. She was also the Commandant of VAD No. 78, in Durham.

Mr Joseph **Crosby** lived and worked at Brancepeth Castle between 3 December 1914 and 28 February 1919, as a full-time house carpenter.

Mrs **De Burg** lived at Quarry Hill and worked at Brancepeth Castle between 27 June 1917 and 29 July 1917 as a part-time nurse.

Miss Dorothy **Dodd** lived and worked at Brancepeth Castle between 3 December 1914 and 1 July 1916 as a part-time kitchen maid and private servant.

Mrs **Durham** lived in Brancepeth and worked at Brancepeth Castle between 21 July 1915 and 12 October 1916 as a part-time nurse.

Mrs Anne **Fillingham** lived at Swiss Cottage, North Road, and worked at Brancepeth Castle between 18 May 1917 and 8 November 1917 as a part-time nurse.

Miss Katherine **Firth** lived at The Vicarage, Esh Winning, Durham and worked at Brancepeth Castle as a part-time nurse between 15 June 1918 and 18 October 1918.

The **Freeman** sisters, Edith and Mary, worked on their father's farm before the war, so had been used to long hours and strenuous work for most of their lives. Besides their parents, Richard and Mary, there were their brothers, Arthur, Frank and Percy as well as another sister, Lily. By the time they started work at Brancepeth Castle they were both twenty-one years of age. Miss Edith Freeman lived at South Brandon Farm, Crook, Durham, and worked at Brancepeth Castle between 15 February 1916 and 25 October 1916, as an officer involved in nursing on a part-time basis. Miss Mary Freeman lived at South Brandon Farm, Crook, Durham, and worked at Brancepeth Castle between 22 August 1917 and 4 March 1917 as a part-time officer engaged in nursing duties.

Mrs Ethel **Gemmell** was from Scotland, her home being at 62 Kelvingrove Street in Glasgow. She worked on a full-time basis at Brancepeth Castle, between 22 March 1915 and 28 February 1919 as a qualified nurse, whose weekly wage was twenty-five shillings and two pence.

Miss Ruth **Genner** lived at Princess Street, Langley Moor, and worked at Brancepeth Castle between 21 July 1915 and 12 October 1916, as a part time nurse, with her rank being that of an officer.

The Honourable Eustace Scott **Hamilton-Russell** OBE, lived at Stoke Lodge in Ludlow and worked at Brancepeth Castle, where he was the full-time Hospital Commandant between 3 December 1914 and 15 March 1919.

The Honourable Mrs Mary Olive Mary **Hamilton-Russell** was Eustace's wife and the full-time Assistant Commandant at Brancepeth Castle, where she also worked from 3 December 1914 until 15 March 1919.

The Honourable Florence Rachel **Hamilton-Russell** lived at Burwarton, Bridgenorth, and worked at Brancepeth Castle between 22 May 1916 and 15 March 1916, when she was employed as a full-time trained masseuse and as somebody who was skilled in what were known as electrical treatments.

Miss Jessie **Harle** lived at Browney Colliery in Durham and worked at Brancepeth Castle between 21 July 1915 and 12 October 1916, and was employed on a part-time basis to carry out general nursing duties.

Mr Albert **Hattow/Hatton** lived and worked at Brancepeth Castle between 3 December 1914 and 28 February 1919. He worked full-time as help in the kitchen. I describe what he did in this way as his VAD registration card records under the heading of Particulars of Duties just the word 'Pantry'. The website where his details are recorded on, www.redcross.org.uk records his name as being Hattow, but when examining the actual hand-written VAD registration card, his name could in fact be Hatton.

Miss Alice **Henry** lived and worked at Brancepeth Castle between 1 June 1915 and 28 February 1919, and worked full time as a stillroom maid and a private servant. A stillroom would be found in all great houses or castles, and was a distillery room, but not just for alcoholic purposes as the name at first suggests. Medicines, cosmetics and home cleaning products would be prepared there. The room would be used to preserve herbs and flowers from the garden for flavouring food.

Miss Ruth Jane Victoria **Hind** lived with her family at the police station in Meadowfield, which is a village situated about two miles south-west of the City of Durham. Her father, Richard William Hind, was a sergeant in the Durham County Police. Besides her mother

*The old police station in Meadowfield. (Photograph by Sharon Harris)*

*Convalescing soldiers. Although not from either of the Durham VAD Hospitals, they are an example of the distinctive uniforms convalescing soldiers wore whilst they were recuperating. Instead of their normal khaki uniforms, they wore a distinctive uniform of sky-blue jacket with white lapels.*

Elizabeth, and two brothers, Norman, who was twenty years of age and worked as a colliery joiner, and Clive, who was only six years of age, they also had three lodgers. John Arnold Towers, who was a Clerk in Holy Orders, and Ray Hutchinson and Dennis McFadden, who were both local police constables.

Mr **Hudspeth/Hudspith** (the spelling of the name isn't clear), lived and worked at Brancepeth Castle between 1 June 1916 and 28 February 1919, as a part time general hand.

Lady Pauline **Jacobs**, who lived at Quarry Hill in Brancepeth, worked at Brancepeth Castle as a part-time nurse for five months between 6 November 1916 and 30 March 1917.

Mrs Sarah **Johnson** lived at 17 Cumberland Terrace, Willington, and worked at Brancepeth hospital as a part time nurse, between 10

May 1915 and 14 May 1919. Prior to this she had worked as a nurse in Workingham, in Salonika and at the Royal Hospital in Woolwich, making her eminently qualified for her work at Brancepeth Castle.

Miss Agnes **Mersom** lived and worked at Brancepeth Castle, where she worked part-time in the kitchen, although she started off as a private servant. She worked for the VAD between 1 May 1917 and 30 September 1918.

Miss Ethel M. **Middlemiss** lived at The Lodge, Brancepeth and worked at Brancepeth Castle between 10 May 1915 and 12 October 1916 as a part-time nurse.

Miss Ella **Newcombe** lived at Forge Bank Colliery and worked at Brancepeth Castle between 14 November 1916 and 10 February 1919 as a part-time nurse.

Miss Mary **Newcombe** worked at Brancepeth Castle as a nurse between 21 July 1915 and 10 January 1918.

Mrs Mary **Newton** lived at Ashleigh, Dene View, Willington and was employed on nursing duties at Brancepeth Castle between 1 March 1916 and 21 July 1917.

Miss Ethel **Nicholl** lived at 16 Queen Street, Brandon, and worked at Brancepeth Castle, between 3 June 1918 and 21 February 1919, as an officer on the nursing side of things.

The four **Raine** sisters all wanted to do their bit for the war effort in the best way that they knew how, and so it was that they all joined the 7th Durham VAD. Their father, John, was a farmer, and the eldest of their four brothers, also John, worked on the farm with his father. I could find no evidence of their brother having served during the war, even though he would have been twenty-two years of age at the outbreak of the war, but working on a farm was a reserved occupation. Miss Anne Jane Raine lived at Nafferton Farm in Brancepeth and worked at Brancepeth Castle, between 10 May 1915 and 12 October 1916, on general nursing duties. Miss Hilda Raine, also lived at Nafferton Farm, Brancepeth. She was employed on general nursing duties at Brancepeth Castle between 10 May 1915 and 28 February 1919. Miss Mary Hannah Raine of 8 Commercial Street, Willington, worked at Brancepeth Castle between 10 August 1916 and 22 June 1917 on general nursing duties. Miss Sarah Greenwell Raine of Nafferton Farm, Brancepeth, worked at Brancepeth Castle between 12 October 1915 and 30 October 1918, and was employed as a nurse on general nursing duties.

Miss Isa **Robson** lived at 56 Durham Street, Brandon Colliery and worked at Brancepeth Castle between 6 October 1918 and 10 February 1919. She was employed as a nurse on general nursing duties.

Mrs **Robson** lived and worked at Brancepeth Castle as a full-time baker and a charlady, between 3 December 1914 and 28 February 1919.

Miss **Rutter** lived at Willington and worked at Brancepeth Castle between 10 May 1915 and 5 May 1919, and was employed on general nursing duties.

Mrs **Ryder** lived and worked at Brancepeth Castle between 1 March 1915 and 28 February 1919, and was employed as a full-time baker and charlady.

Miss Mary **Sherrington** lived at East Farm in Brandon Village and worked at Brancepeth Castle for only eight months between 22 April 1918 and 20 December 1918, being employed on general nursing duties.

Mrs Amy **Small** lived at 18 Cumberland Terrace, Millington and worked at Brancepeth Castle between 10 April 1916 and 6 June 1919 as a nurse.

Mrs Harriet **Small** lived at 5 Kensington Terrace, Willington and worked at Brancepeth Castle between 10 June 1916 and 28 February 1919 as a nurse.

Miss Anne **Southwell** lived and worked at Brancepeth Castle as a part-time kitchen maid and private servant between 1 July 1916 and 1 July 1918.

Mrs Millicent **Stevenson** lived at Primrose Hill, Newfield, Willington and worked at Brancepeth Castle between 9 November 1914 and 17 February 1918 as a nurse.

Miss Lena **Taylor** lived at Cordilleras House, Richmond, and worked at Brancepeth Castle between 1 January 1918 and 28 February 1919, as a full-time trained nurse, who earned twenty-five shillings and two pence a week.

Miss E **Udell** lived and worked at Brancepeth Castle as a full-time cook and private servant between 3 December 1914 and 28 February 1919.

Miss Annie **Wainer** lived and worked at Brancepeth Castle as a full-time housekeeper and private servant, between 3 December 1914 and 28 February 1919.

Miss Annie **Weeks** lived at Willington House, Willington, and was a Nurse at Brancepeth Castle between 19 June 1915 and 25 January 1917.

Besides those who are named above, there were many more women and men who served throughout the First World War in the VADs at numerous different locations across the country. The work which these individuals did was just as important and they should be remembered accordingly. One such individual was Lilian **Meiklejohn** who lived at 1 Pelaw Terrace, Durham, and worked in the mess room of the Victoria Regis Hospital, 5 Saville Row, London, WC, between May 1917 and February 1919.

CHAPTER 7

# The Aftermath

The Armistice had been signed, the war was over and the world was trying to get back to normality, whatever that would be, in a post-war Great Britain. Russia had had its revolution which saw their Imperial Family dispensed with in the most brutal way possible, and in 1917 France had seen a mass mutiny by its troops, which forced a review of their tactics and the removal of some senior commanders.

The end of the war had most definitely brought changes with it. Ordinary folk were no longer happy just to accept their lot in life: they expected and wanted more. Over 7,000,000 men and women, had enlisted in the British armed forces during the First World War, but this figure, huge as it was, almost paled in to insignificance when compared to the number of relatives who were connected to those individuals. There were an awful lot of people who were directly or indirectly affected by the First World War, which remains one of the deadliest conflicts in human history. The total number killed and wounded from all sides is estimated as being seventeen million dead with a further twenty million who were wounded. Out of these, Great Britain had just over 700,000 of its men killed in the army and 32,000 men in the navy.

On 11 November 1918, the news that people had been waiting and praying for in communities across the country had finally arrived. In Durham City the news spread like wildfire, with Union Jack flags suddenly appearing from nearly every building for as far as the eye could see. Although a spontaneous reaction to the enormity and suddenness of the news, it was almost as if the display of national pride and fervour was orchestrated in some magical way. The Cathedral and church bells rang out loud and proud, their collective sound bringing joy and happiness to everybody. People were in the streets, singing and rejoicing, nearly all of them either holding or adorned with miniature flags and rosettes, even the cars and other vehicles were adorned in a similar way.

The city's Mayor, Alderman George Henderson Proctor, who had only been elected the previous week, quickly gathered the members of the council and other prominent members of the local community, and in the afternoon there was a massive coming together of people in the Market Square, in anticipation of war end celebrations. Mr Proctor was a Conservative and had been with the council since 1897. He had previously been the city's mayor back in 1904 and the following year was made an alderman.

The band of the Northumberland Fusiliers were also present to join in the celebrations, playing patriotic and uplifting music. The Mayor, the Mayoress, the Deputy Mayor, Bishop Welldon, the Dean of Durham, Mr Broderick Dale the High Sheriff of the County of Durham, Mrs Axel Morck, the Chaplain, Reverend Dr Dawson Walker, along with others officially confirmed that the Armistice had been signed, the war was over, and the killing had finally stopped. The Mayor called out, 'Thank God,' adding, 'It is to the honour and credit of our Empire. We give our everlasting thanks to the brave lads of our Army and Navy, who have brought the Huns to their knees. God save the King.' After the Mayor's comments the regimental band of the Northumberland Fusiliers, played the National Anthem, to loud applause.

The Dean of Durham was the next to address the crowds:

Thanks be to God for what was, humanly speaking, the near prospect of the end of the terrible world struggle. We must remember that the billows of the ocean of war would be felt in a measure inside the harbour of peace. The prospect of peace, both from the European and world-wide aspect, and from the conditions that would evoke in our English life at home, was a prospect which would demand all the long inherited instincts of the English race, at once for liberty and order, and would call with peculiar insistence for the unselfish loyalty and patriotism of parties, classes and interests.

I am proud and glad to take part in this day's celebration. It is perhaps the greatest day in all history [I am not quite sure that's how German people would have viewed it]. I do not think it is a day for noisy rejoicing, but it is a day for solemn thanksgiving. We acknowledge the providence of Almighty God in delivering our nation and the Empire from the worst of all dangers. We remember with profound gratitude and conviction the men of this country and of the colonies and of all Allied countries, who have died in the war, and we pledge ourselves at this time, when the British Empire has attained a pinnacle unknown before by our own resolve, and purpose to make our nation and our Empire's future not unworthy of the great victory which has been won. May the blessing of the highest rest upon our nation and Empire, now and always.

After a few more addresses the revellers joined together in singing, 'Praise God from whom all Blessings flow.' The crowds in the Market Square were swelled somewhat at lunchtime, when all the City's schoolchildren were not just given the rest of the day off, but the rest of the week.

In reality it was the strangest of days. The Dean of Durham had said, it was not a day for noisy rejoicing, but a day for solemn thanksgiving, but in part it was for both. The war was finally over, and rightly so it was a time to celebrate a great victory, but hand in hand with that went the thanks that after just over four years of bloody war, it was finally over, and that the killing had finally stopped. People present in the crowd that day would have had mixed emotions. Some of them would have lost loved ones in the war and would still be mourning their own personal loss. At least for them there would have been the knowledge that the sacrifice their loved ones had made had not been in vain. There would have been sadness and joy all rolled in to one, each and every person there present, dealing with their own separate set of emotions. Neighbours standing shoulder to shoulder, one knowing that their loved one was never coming home, and that for them, all there would be would be memories and the name of their loved one commemorated on a memorial. Others had the joy of looking forward to the homecoming of the person that they loved, whether as husband, father, brother or son. How surreal that so many emotions were swirling round Durham City Market Square, that Monday morning back in November 1918.

And so it was that the world returned to what it had once been, but not in every sense. The madness of war had finally stopped, that was welcomed with open arms by one and all, but there was now an air of expectation about a better tomorrow and a brighter future for everybody. The sacrifice which had been made by so many had to mean something, if it were to have any purpose and value.

The people didn't want to hear any more political excuses. It was the working man who had borne the brunt of the war, certainly when it came to the numbers of men who had been killed and wounded. In return they wanted to see tangible rewards, not just the rhetoric of empty words. In Durham City, housing was one of the main issues which urgently needed addressing.

The City of Durham, like 263 other towns and cities up and down the country, was presented with a tank for its wartime efforts in recognition of the 'splendid response by the citizens of Durham, to the various appeals made for war loans,' and to commemorate the war. Some people even thought that it was intended to be a kind or war memorial. Tank No. 2783 duly arrived in the city on 10 June 1919, having arrived at Gilesgate Goods Station, after a fortnight's train journey, straight from the battlefields of France. The truth of the matter was that with the war now over, the Government had a surplus of military hardware that they no longer had any need for, and giving them away in this manner was actually a less expensive way of getting rid of it, and if towns and cities up and down the country felt better for having one in their midst, then all the better.

It had been decided that the tank was going to be situated at the city's Wharton Park, but to get it there, it first had to be moved by train to North Road station, where on 17 June 1919 the 27-ton beast was unloaded before being driven to its finally resting place, at a pedestrian speed of four miles per hour. What damage it did to the local roads can only be guessed at, as they were designed at a time when a horse and trap were the kings of the highway. The slow speed of the tank was a blessing in disguise as the journey from North Road station to Wharton Park wasn't entirely without incident, but thankfully there was no major damage to report.

With the tank was the actual man who had been in command of it when it had been on active service in France, Captain Walter Frederick Farrar, who had been awarded the Military Cross in 1918 for taking out a German machine-gun position in his Mark IV tank. He had first arrived in France on 9 November 1915. Before the war he had been a bank clerk in London, and when the war started he joined No. 3 Company, Inns of Court OTC. When he applied for his service medals in June 1920, his home address was shown as being in Trinidad.

With the local dignitaries having made their individual speeches, the celebrations were brought to end with the singing of the National Anthem, which was sung passionately and with vigour by all those present. A lot of the tanks that were presented in this way, not only hadn't seen any kind of action, but hadn't even left the country. The furthest they had ever been was to the Tank Corp's depot at Bovington in Dorset, where they had been used for training.

A lot of the tanks that were presented in this way ended up being sold off for scrap in later years. The memory and excitement of their arrival, had long since dissipated in to nothing more than a recollection of a bygone era. A lot of the tanks, having been battered by the elements for more than fifteen years, had become rusty and unsightly, and in some cases, a safety hazard to the young children, who clambered all over them on a daily basis. The one in Wharton Park was one of those that had become a bit of an eyesore, and was going to now start costing money to repair it. Its future had been a topic of discussion for more than ten years, before Durham City Council finally decided on 7 October 1936 that the tank should be sold off.

## CHAPTER 8

# First World War Memorials in Durham

❖

**Durham School**
There is a war memorial which commemorates those who were killed during the First World War, who were either masters or ex-pupils of the Durham School, the vast majority of whom were officers. It is located in the school's chapel and is in the form of eight pillars, which contains a total of ninety-eight names:

Charles Young Adamson
Robert William Adamson
William Boyd
Robert Hugh Burkitt
Charles Patrick Caesar
Thomas William Callinan
William Charlton
Herbert Golightly Constantine
Arthur James Dingle
Cave Bradburne Dodds
Ronald Dundas Falconar-Stewart
Henry Harley Fownes
Peter Gedge
John Gibson
Ernest John Robinson Briggs Gooderham

Francis Douglas Adamson
Newton Wynn Apperley
Alexander Buchannan
Fassett Arborin Burnett
Frank Clagget Caird
Victor Francis Carr
Arthur Stewart Churchyard
George Edwin Craven
Hugh John Dingle
Walter Melbourne Dodds
Cuthbert Fosbrooke
Norman Gawan-Taylor
Reginald Claud Moline Gee
Herbert Reginald Gladstone
Max Grevil Jones

Humphrey Blaikie Goudie
Wynne Austin Guest-Williams
William Hall
George Kenneth Hampton
Joseph William Smith Hird
Cyril Gordon Hosking
George Alan William Hulley
Noel Forbes Humphreys
Gwynne Jacob
Frederick Henry Lawson
Ralph Hawksworth Legard
Frederick Cecil Longden
William Marley Horace Frost Marris
Alfred William Maughan
William Miles Morant
William Noel Jobson Moscrop
Nathaniel Clark Nielson
Frederick Lisle Newstead
Frank Paterson
Ryde Guild Rayner
Basil Hulton Richardson
Bertram Langhorne Robinson
George Sydney Robinson
Gerald Gloag Sadler
Herbert Stewart
Harold Kenyon Temperley
Spencer Thomson
Alick Todd
James Douglas Tombs
Ernest Wilberforce Trevor
John Pattinson Walker
Bertram Howard Wodeham
Thomas Tweddell
Harold Forbes Clarke Winch

Ronald William Craig Gunn
Ronald Lidderdale Guy
Bernard St. George Hamilton
Gerald Montague Hedley
William Noel Hodgson
Herbert Edward Hosking
John Theodore Gordon Humphreys
John Edgar Hirst Hurst
George Kirkhouse
Ian Alister Leeson
Ernest William Longden
Bertram Lionel Maddison
Hubert Graham Hamilton Marshall
Alfred Frederick Maynard
Arthur Morgan
Thomas Muir
George Newby
Nowell Oxland
Idris Knox Patton Mowbray Procter
Henry William Ternent Reed
Martin James Richardson
Charles Lawson Robinson
Charles Oxendale Robson
Arthur Duncombe Shafto
Hilton Roberts Telford
Arthur Weatherhead Thompson
Kirton Tindle
John George Todd
Francis Edward Stevenson Townsend

There are, sadly, too many names on the list to look at every one of them in detail, but I will take a closer look at a selection of them. A lot of these names are extremely unusual, and not too many of them have survived the test of time, or appear today in any great numbers. A lot of young men who are now sadly names of a lost generation.

Fassett Arbouin **Burnett**, originally enlisted as a private (3010) in the Honourable Artillery Company, but ended up as a gunner (319435) in the 63rd Company, Royal Garrison Artillery. He was killed in action on 1 August 1918. He was a New Zealander by birth, having been born in Auckland in 1896. He is buried at the Pieta Military Cemetery in Malta, which is located in Triq id-Duluri, near Valletta. There are the bodies of 1,303 Commonwealth soldiers buried in the cemetery who were killed during the First World War. Up until May 1917, when Germany increased her submarine activity in the area of the Mediterranean, the islands of Malta and Gozo had been extensively used by military hospitals and convalescent depots, which treated more than 135,000 wounded soldiers, mainly from the fighting in Gallipoli.

Herbert Golightly **Constantine** was only eighteen years of age when he was killed in action on 2 June 1918, whilst serving as a lance corporal (36234) in France with 'C' Company 7th Battalion, Border Regiment. He is buried in the Aucheux British Cemetery in the Somme region of France. There are a total of 150 Allied servicemen buried in the cemetery from the First World War, a number of whom were killed in the period of April to August 1918, during the last German offensive of the war.

Newton Wynn **Apperley**, is one of the names recorded on the school's memorial as having been killed during the war. Newton served in the Royal Navy during the war, at the beginning of which he was only nineteen years of age, having been born in Durham on 28 October 1894. He was a probationary midshipman and his service number was 2104. Having searched his name on the Commonwealth War Graves Commission website for those killed during the First World War, I could find no trace of him. I then carried out a similar search on the website, www.naval-history.net, once again finding nobody of this name showing as having been a casualty of the First World War. I then looked up the National Probate calendar which showed his middle name spelt, 'Wynne'. In it, his father, who also had the name of Newton Wynne Apperley, was shown as being a retired Royal Navy captain.

This also showed his date of death as being 20 June 1918. He was buried at the now-redundant St Mary-le-Bow Church, in Durham. For a period of time in the years leading up to the First World War, Newton spent a period of time in Australia, having arrived in Sydney on 11 December 1912 on board the SS *Mersey*, although he was back in England and was a midshipman in the Royal Naval Reserve by 1 September 1914. On the 1901 Census Newton's surname is actually spelt Applesley, although on the very same entry his parents name is clearly shown as being Applerley. All of the above name variations and different permutations, show just how difficult it can sometimes be to research individuals with a degree of absolute certainty. Newton had an elder brother, Alan Wynne Apperley, who also served during the First World War, Initially as a second lieutenant in the 18th Battalion, Durham Light Infantry, and latterly as a captain in the Royal Engineers. He first arrived in France on 12 July 1916. It is known that on 20 August 1921, Alan was living at South End in Durham. Having survived the war, he lived to the ripe old age of eighty-four, passing away in March 1970 in his beloved Durham.

Bernard St George **Hamilton** was actually born in Lowestoft in Suffolk on 24 January 1892. When he left Durham School, he continued his studies at the Halifax Technical College. At the age of twenty-one, he enlisted in the Glasgow Highlanders in 1913. With the outbreak of the war, it wasn't long before he found himself serving in France, arriving there with the British Expeditionary Force in October 1914. Three months later, in January 1915, he was back home in England having been diagnosed with trench foot, the scourge of many a British Tommy. Once he was sufficiently recovered he returned to France, but returned home and received a commission with the 13th Battalion, The Highland Light Infantry, in October 1915, and was then attached to the Machine Gun Corps, being sent to Grantham in Lincolnshire to complete his training. He married Ethel Margaret Swinnerton on 14 August 1916, before returning to France for a third time, two months later in October. Bernard was killed in action during fighting at Oppy Wood on 28 June 1917 whilst leading an attack into a captured German trench. At the time of his death he was a lieutenant with the 15th Company, Machine Gun Corps. Although a successful attack by the British, by the end of the day they had suffered a total of 452 casualties. An earlier attack on Oppy Wood, had taken place on 3

May 1917, as part of the Battle of the Scarpe, when British forces incurred 2,417 casualties, whilst being repelled by German units.

A fellow officer wrote a letter to Bernard's wife, Ethel: 'You may well be proud of your husband; he was always fearless, loved by his men and popular among the whole division. He was a fine officer and always did his work well. We all miss him more than I can say', while a second officer wrote: 'He was always so bright and cheery, and ready to do more than his share of work, and that he was loved and admired by everyone. I've never seen men so upset as his section is about it. He was buried at dead of night where he fell, a fitting place for such a warrior.' Another comrade wrote the following: 'Bernard would go out in his usual cheery way; we all knew he couldn't be anything else. Many will miss him; none do so more than his own men, who have had the good fortune to have him to command them.' It would appear that Bernard was an exceptional young man who was a natural leader of men, a life sadly extinguished because of the war and his dedication to his job and the men under his command. Although buried soon after his death, the actual location of his grave was lost and after the war his body was not recovered. Instead his name is one of the 35,000 which were subsequently commemorated on the Arras Memorial.

Cuthbert **Fosbrooke** started the war in the Middlesex Regiment as Private 2681. He later transferred to the Army Cyclist Corps as a private (20543), before receiving a commission as a second lieutenant in the 22nd (Pioneer) Battalion, Durham Light Infantry, on 24 January 1917. He was killed in action six months later, on 19 July 1917, aged twenty-five. He is buried in the Dickebusch New Military Cemetery Extension, in the West-Vlaanderen region of Belgium. The 1911 Census showed Cuthbert, who was an articled clerk to an accountant, living at The Vicarage, 408 Hartshill Road, Stoke On Trent, Staffordshire. His father, Arthur Middleton Fosbrooke, was a Clerk in Holy Orders. With his mother, Jane, two sisters and two servants, Cuthbert must have been well looked-after.

William Noel Jobson **Moscrop** was a married man, having wed Sarah Ellen Eaton in February 1915. He was killed in action on 6 November 1917 whilst serving in Belgium. At the time of his death he was a private (54818) in the 127th Company, Machine Gun Corps, although he had originally enlisted as a private (25774) in the Border Regiment. He is buried in the Coxyde Military Cemetery, in Koksijde Arrondissement Veurne in the West-Vlaanderen region of Belgium. William had an elder brother, Robert John Moscrop, and there was a Robert Moscrop, who served with the Northumberland Fusiliers as a private (7/2249) and an acting sergeant, who had been awarded the Military Cross. It is possible that this could be one and the same man.

Bertram Langhorne **Robinson** was a captain in the 4th Company, 50th Divisional Train, Army Service Corps, first arriving in France on 17 April 1915. When he died on 6 September 1917, he was forty-three years of age. His sister, Mrs Louise Pinkney, of 2 Manor House Road, Jesmond, Newcastle-upon-Tyne, applied for his wartime service medals on 17 October 1921.

**Durham County Council War Memorial**
The idea for a local war memorial in Durham, was that of the Local Government Officers' Association, who applied to the County Council's Finance Committee, for the funding of a war memorial in October 1919. One year later and with the wheels of bureaucracy having completed a full circuit, permission was finally granted for a brass tablet to be put on display at the Shire Hall, listing the names of all Council staff who had lost their lives as a result of the war. Furthermore they also agreed that a memorial book containing the names of all Council staff who went off to fight in the war, should also be produced. It was another nine months before the brass tablets were finally unveiled on 27 July 1921, at a cost of £230.

The present war memorial, which is situated at County Hall in Durham City, is not the first war memorial that the city has had, the original one having been on public display at the Shire Hall. The County Hall War Memorial commemorates the names of the 122 men who prior to the First World War, had been employed by the County Council, but when the war started went off to fight, and sadly didn't survive. During the course of the war 1,134 men who were County Council employees left to go off and fight in the war. Out of these a staggering 823 of them, nearly 75 per cent, were teachers.

Here are the names of the men who are commemorated on the memorial and rightly remembered for eternity for the sacrifice which each and every one of them made.

Allen, Francis
Armstrong, Joseph
Arnett, William
Ash, Oswald Charles
Ashworth, James Francis Gordon
Atkinson, Joseph Hewitson
Axtell, Alfred John
Baker, W.
Barclay, John
Barr, John William
Barton, John
Bates, William
Bayles, William H.
Beardmore, Norman
Bell, Thomas Haddon
Bennett, Norman
Booth, John George
Bower, Gordon
Bradley, William Hall
Brock, Alfred Lawrence
Brown, Christopher
Brown, Thomas
Brown, William Herbert
Brown, William Lionel Gerald
Brown, William T.
Buffham, Harry Augustus
Chambers, Norman Wilson
Chester, Arthur
Chipchase, Henry
Clancy, Arthur Daniel
Clark, John George
Clark, Percy
Collin, Samuel Story
Cook, James Edward
Cook, Percy
Coon, Arthur

Corker, Richard Robson
Corner, Arthur Henry
Cosgrove, Albert Bruce
Crabb, Jacob
Crawford, George
Crawshaw, Charles Neville
Curry, Ralph
Deighton, Ralph
Drummond, Harry
Duke, John
Elliot, John Oliver
Elsdon, Ingram Thomas
Fairless, Edward
Ferguson, Thomas
Flavill, Joseph Cyril
Ford, Basil
Forrest, Wilson
Foster, Robert William
Francis, Idris Theodore Trefor
Frankton, John Bernard
Fullerton, Matthew
Gibson, Matthew
Groves, Robert Lishman
Guy, Joseph
Harrison, Thomas Richard Stafford
Hedger, Walter Stanley
Heslop, John Glenwright
Heslop, William,
Hetherington, Arthur
Hogan, John William
Hogg, Robert
Hook, John
Hoole, William David
Horn, John
Hetherington Huggins, John Warrick

Jameson, Richard
Jones, Robert
King, Henry
Lawson, James Heslop
Macdonald, Kenneth
McPherson, George
Metcalfe, Alexander John
Middlemass, George Edward
Minks, Thomas
Moore, Henry
Moore John J.
Noon, Gilbert
Parker, Anthony Edward Linton
Pattinson, Edward Fidler
Peadon, Harold Thomas
Pratt, Thomas Smith
Prudham, Thomas Pearson
Pyburn, Thomas Bowerbank
Pybus, Robert
Richardson, Alexander Lister
Richardson, William Edward
Richmond, Oliver
Rigg, Tyson
Rivers, George Stephenson
Robertson, Archibald Wilson
Robinson, Thomas Naylor
Robson, John William
Robson, Robert Henry
Robson, Robert Ramsey

Robson, Thomas
Rowell, Hugh Fraser
Rowell, John Frederick
Rudd, Michael Whitton
Sanderson, Christopher
Sanderson, James Johnson
Seed, Frederick
Shepherd, Stanley
Shortridge, Lawrence
Sinclair, John Hanson
Smith, Arthur Edward
Smith, Thomas Henry
Soulsby, Richard Rennie
Stanfield, Thomas William
Stobbs, Harry Henry
Stockdale, William Henry
Taylor, Edwin
Tiffin, Thomas Henry
Turnbull, William Hall
Turner, Arthur
Vickers, Arthur Dodds Lewis
Wake, Joseph Pyke
Walker, William Gordon Brumwell
Watson, Joseph Matthew
Watson, Sydney
Waud, Ernest Henry
Werry, Harvey Simpson
Wilson, Edward Ridley
Wood, Joseph Ramsay Curry
Wood, William
Yeaman, Charles Henry
Yule, Robert

## Durham Cathedral

Besides the Main Durham County Memorial to commemorate the names of those who lost their lives in the First World War, there are many smaller ones, simply naming individuals or men from a particular regiment, such as the Durham Light Infantry. Many of these can be found in churches in the form of plaques, crosses, memorials, books of remembrance and rolls of honour, everyone just as important as the next.

There is a memorial in the shape of a column situated in the grounds of Durham Cathedral, although that wasn't its first resting place. It was unveiled by the Lord Lieutenant, the Marquess of Londonderry, on Saturday, 24 November 1928, which in relation to most other memorials, across Great Britain, was quite late with most being erected in the early 1920s. The cost of most was, in most cases, met by public donations.

The only inscription on the memorial is on the concrete base which simply reads, '1914–1918.' The memorial does not contain the names of any of the men from Durham City who were killed during the course of the First World War. It was designed by Professor Charles H. Reilly, who was a lecturer at the University of Liverpool, and it was sculptured by Mr H. Tyson Smith, also from Liverpool.

There is also a War Memorial Cross in the grounds of the Cathedral. Inside the Cathedral are a number of Stained Glass windows one of these represents the nine Choristers who lost their lives during the First World War. Underneath the window is a stone panel, which sits between two half-rounded pillars, and contains the names of the nine men who lost their lives. Below the list of names is an inscription in Latin. This memorial wasn't unveiled until 19 September 1935.

The Cathedral is also home to a memorial in honour of the officers and men of the Durham Light Infantry who lost their lives during the course of the war. It does not bear any names, just this simple inscription:

> To the glory of God and in honour of the officers, warrant officers, non-commissioned officers and men of the Durham Light Infantry, who laid down their lives in the Great War, A.D. 1914-1918. This chapel has been set apart as a Regimental Memorial and as a monument of the gratitude of their fellow

countrymen whom they inspired by their devotion, sustained by their courage, and delivered by their sacrifice.

There is also a Book of Remembrance for the men of the Durham Light Infantry who were killed during the First World War. It sits in a glass fronted wooden case. The book contains the names of some 12,606 men. The pages of the book are turned on a daily basis.

The College of St Hild and St Bede, which is part of the University of Durham, has a War Memorial Cross that commemorates those who fell in the Great War, located in its grounds and which was unveiled on 29 May 1922 by Lieutenant Colonel J.R. Ritson, who was the officer commanding the 8th Battalion, Durham Light Infantry.

*The Hild-Bede College War Memorial. (Photograph by Dr Robert O'Hara)*

*City of Durham Roll of Honour. (Photograph by Laurie Rampling)*

**City of Durham Roll of Honour**
There is also a Roll of Honour which includes the names of the 360 men from the City of Durham who lost their lives during the First World War. This is currently located in Durham Town Hall.

The following article appeared in the *Yorkshire Post & Leeds Intelligencer* on Thursday 3 March 1921, concerning the unveiling of the 'Durham City War Memorial.'

> In Durham Town Hall yesterday, the Mayor Mr W. Thwaites, unveiled a scroll memorial to the men from the city who fell in the war.
>
> The Earl of Durham, who addressed the gathering, said the men of Durham had carried forward all the best and noblest traditions of their county. Their courage, their loyalty and their determination to carry on through all the difficulties and dangers of the war was an honour to the city and the county. Their memory must be honoured not only by remembering what they did for their fellow citizens, but by trying to help our country to attain that prosperity and happiness for which they fought and died. Differences should not be exaggerated, but diminished and dispelled, and all should unite in friendly co-operation and wise provision and foresight for the future.

The names of the 360 men are recorded below. Most of them were in the Army with some of them being in the Royal Navy, but what is interesting is the many different regiments that they represented. A large percentage of them served with the many different battalions of the Durham Light Infantry whilst others served in the Essex Regiment and the Winnipeg Rifles.

Every single one of them brave and heroic individuals. Some of the surnames appear on more than four occasions: Stephenson, Tait, Maddison, Fenwick, Heron, Smith and Walton.

| | | | |
|---|---|---|---|
| Capt. Adamson C.Y., 8th R.S.F. | L Sgt Blakey W., 17th Miss R. | Sgt Carr C.D., N.Z. Rifle Bde | Pte Curry J., N.F. |
| Pte Ainsley G., R.A.S.C. | Cpl Bone J.G., 8th Somerset L.I. | Capt Carr V.R., R.G.A. | Lt Christopher R., T.C. |
| - Ainsley R., 6th D.L.I. | Pte Bone W.S., 8th D.L.I. | Sgt Carrick W.W., W.W. 18th D.L.I. | Pte Davey A., 5th D.L.I. |
| L Cpl Anderson T.F.G., 3rd D.L.I. | - Bowes J., N.F. | Dvr Carter E., Tank Corps. | - Davey T.E., N.F. |
| Midshipman Apperley N.W., R.N. | - Bowes R., D.L.I. | - Casey O., R.A.S.C. | - Davison A., 3rd Cam Hlrs |
| Pte Appleton G.W., 5th D.F. | - Bowes W., | Pte Chapelow J., 2nd D&D Regt | - Davison J., 10th Hussars |
| Gnr Arnold W.H., R.F.A. | Lieut Boyd W., 8th D.L.I. | - Chapman J., | - Dawson E.W.S., W.G.C. |
| Pte Atkinson R., Scottish Rifles. | Pte Brass J., Manchester R. | - Cherry W.R., 3rd W.G.C. | - Dent S., D.L.I. |
| - Atkinson T.R., 18th N.F. | - Breese T., 6th N.F. | - Cheshire W., Ref Mar L.I. | - Dews R., 7th Yorks. |
| L Cpl Aves H.G., A.I.F. | - Brooke J., D.L.I. | - Cheston T., 5th E.Yorks. | - Dixon E., K.O.S.B. |
| | Capt Brown A.N., W.C. D.L.I. | Cpl Chicken W.R., 2nd Yorks. | - Dixon S.F., 1st Royal Marns |
| Pte Baker A., 2nd N.F. | L Cpl Brown C., W.G. Corps. | S Sgt Matchrisp T., 8th D.L.I. | - Dobinson . N.F. |
| - Baker T., 18th E.Yorks. | Cpl Brown H., 9th N.F. | Pte Churnside J., 7th Border Rgt | - Dodds J., 22nd D.L.I. |
| H.B.Banks G.W., R.N. | Pte Brown J., 6th Yorks. | - Clapham W.H., 10th E. Lancs. | Cpl Donaldson W., R.F.A. |
| Pte Barker R., 6th Yorks. | - Brown J.V. De L.,6th yorks | - Clement A.H., R.Fusiliers. | Pte Dowd J., R.I.R. |
| Cpl Barnes A., 12th D.L.I. | - Brydon R., | Gnr Clement W., R.F.A. | - Duffy W., York & Lancs Rgt |
| Pte Barron J.R., 9th Yorks. | Cpl Bryson R.H., R.F.A. | Pte Coatham J.R., 18th D.L.I. | |
| - Barron J.W., - - | - Bulmer J., R.I.Rifles | Stoker Cochrane J., R.N. | Pte Eales E.J., 18th D.L.I. |
| Pte Beeby J.N., 2nd D.L.I. | Pte Burrell R.P. | Pte Coffin S., R.A.W.C. | - Ebdy R., R.N. |
| - Beeby N., N.F. | L Cpl Burton R.H., 2nd Worcester R. | - Collins W., 11th 8th W.B. Rgt | Pte Elliott E., 20th D.L.I. |
| - Bell G., 1st K.O.S.B. | Pte Bush J., N.F. | - Cosgrove A., | L Cpl Elliott R., Loyal N Lancs |
| L Cpl Bell W., 5th West Yorks. | Pte Butterworth W.H.,6th D.L.I. | Eng Artificer Coxon E.W., R.N. | Pte Elliott W., R.A.W.C. |
| Cpl Berry N.C., 18th Hussars. | | Pte Coyne R.E., Coldstr 6ds | - Evans E., 18th D.L.I. |
| Pte Bilton E., 18th D.L.I. | Midshipman Cadle E.G., R.N. | Cpl Craggs W.G., 7th Yorks. | - Evans J.J., 16th D.L.I. |
| - Birkett T., - - | Capt Cadle L.W., Aust. I.F. | Pte Cranmer T.D., Y. & L. Rgt | - Ewbank T., 18th D.L.I. |
| - Blagdon J., 9th Yorks. | Lieut Callinan T.W., 8th D.L.I. | Bombs Sgt Crombie J.C., 1st E.Yorks. | |
| Q.M.Burnett E.J., R.N. | Pte Carr C.E., A.I.F. | Sgt Cross C.T., 1st D.L.I. | Pte Fairley G., 10th D.L.I. |
| | | L Cpl Culbert W., | L Cpl Fairley P., D.L.I. |
| | | Pte Cunningham S., 19th D.L.I. | |

| | | | |
|---|---|---|---|
| Pte Farthing J., 12th D.L.I. | - Goodyear C.W., 20th D.L.I. | Pte Heslop J., D.L.I. | Pte Keeble E.W., 19th D.L.I. |
| - Farthing P., 7th K.O.Y.L.I. | Dvr Gray G., R.F.A. | - Hodgson A., | Trooper Kelly J., 6th D. Guards |
| - Featherstonhaugh W., 8th D.L.I. | Pte Greenwell G.R., A.O.C. | - Hodgson J., 2nd Yorks. | Pte Kerwin A., 9th Yorks |
| - Featherstonhaugh W.S., - | - Grieveson T., 20th D.L.I. | - Hodgson H., 8th D.L.I. | Keys Wells W.F., |
| Pte Fenwick A., 4th N.F. | | L Cpl Hogg T., 15th D.L.I. | Pte King T., 2nd N.F. |
| - Fenwick A., D.L.I. | Pte Hall A., 5th D.L.I. | Pte Holland E.W., 8th D.L.I. | - Kirk H., 2nd D.L.I. |
| - Fenwick A., 15th D.L.I. | - Hanley Walt., | - Holland W.B., 5th Yorks. | - Kirwin J., W.R. Regt |
| - Fenwick W., 8th D.L.I. | - Hanley Michl., 1st N.F. | - Holliday J.L., 5th D.L.I. | |
| Sgt Finan W., N.F. | Sapper Hardy S., R.E. | - Hook J., | Pte Laing J.A., W.O.C. |
| Pte Fisher R., 25th N.F. | Pte Hargreaves C., | - Hook W., | - Lambert R., R.I.R. |
| - Fletcher J., | - Harker T., 11th D.L.I. | - Hopper R., Tank Corps. | Sgt Le Count A.G., 1st N.F. |
| Gnr Flowers J., R.F.A. | - Harland R., 7th E.Yorks. | - Hopper T., | Pte Le Count L.A., 9th Yorks. |
| Pte Foley E., N.F. | - Harrington J., 8th Lab Corps | - Hudson W., 8th D.L.I. | - Lee A., D.L.I. |
| Co Sgt Maj. Forrest W., 18th D.L.I. | Gnr Harris G.O., R.F.A. | - Humble T., 25th N.F. | L Cpl Lee K., 21st Canadians. |
| Capt Forster G.R., 19th D.L.I. | Pte Harris J.W., | - Humble R.A., | Pte Liddell G., |
| Pte Foster G., - | - Harrison G.H., 22nd D.L.I. | | - Loch W., 15th D.L.I. |
| - Fox J., 4th D L I | - Hart T., 7th Yorks. | Pte Ingles H., E.Yorks. | L Cpl Lockey F.D., 18th D.L.I. |
| - Fox J.H., 23rd N.F. | Sgt Hauxwell G.W., 7th D.L.I. | | Pte Lockwood T., 15th D.L.I. |
| Gnr Freeman A., R.F.A. | - Hawkins J., 8th D.L.I. | Pte Jackson W., 8th D.L.I. | - Loftus T., |
| | - Hayes E.P., 19 Lincs. | - Jarvis T.W., 8th D.L.I. | - Lumsden K., 8th D.L.I. |
| Pte Gaffney P., N.F. | Cpl Hazelgreaves W.,6th E Kents. | - Jarvis W., 1st Loyal N Lancs | |
| - Gallagher J., Q.O.Y. Dragoons | - Heckles L.S., Scottish Horse. | - Johnson A., | Capt Macfarlane R., R.N. |
| - Gill J., | Pte Hendrick J., 15th D.L.I. | - Johnson E., R.F.A. | Cpl Madden J.K., R.F.A. |
| - Gilroy H., N.F. | L Cpl Heron A.H., - - | - Johnson J., 16th N.F. | Pte Maddison E., 8th D.L.I. |
| - Gilvey J., | - Heron C.E., R.E. | - Johnson J.J., Labour Corps. | 2nd Lt Maddison A., 7th Norfolk Rgt |
| - Gleason G., | Pte Heron H., 11th Royal Scots. | - Johnson J.T., 15th D.L.I. | Lt Col Maddison P.L., 2nd Yorks |
| - Golightly W.D., 16th N.F. | - Heron W., 4th London Rgt | A.B. Johnson N., R.N. | Pte Markham T., 15th D.L.I. |

| | | | | | |
|---|---|---|---|---|---|
| Lt | Marshall W. | 8th D.L.I. | Cpl | Norwood W. | 27th N.F. |
| L Cpl | Mason J. | 1st N.F. | Pte | O'Connor A. | 8th D.L.I. |
| Pte | Maxwell J. | D.L.I. | Bombr | Oliver J., M.M. | R.F.A. |
| Lt | Maynard H.F. | R.N.V.R. | Pte | Oughton J. | 1st N.F. |
| Pte | McDermott | D.L.I. | Master at Arms Parry F.G. | | R.N. |
| " | McGregor G.F. | 22nd D.L.I. | Pte | Parry G.V. | K.O.Y.L.I. |
| Sgt | McNamara A. | Yorks | " | Peacock G.W.P. Can. Ex. Force | |
| Pte | Mearis F.B. | 7th W. Yorks | L Cpl | Pedwell J. | 8th D.L.I. |
| " | Meewley | 8th N.F. | Pte | Pedwell W. | " " |
| " | Melia John. | | Cpl | Pennington J. | 13th N.F. |
| " | Melia Jos. | | Pte | Perrin H. | 15th London Rgt |
| " | Metcalfe J. | M.G.C. | " | Peverall T. | 8th E. Yorks |
| " | Minto B. | 1st Cam. Highlanders | Gnr | Phillips W.E. | R.F.A. |
| " | Mitchell E. | 5th Shropshire | Pte | Pickering G.A. | 5th N.F. |
| " | Moore A. | | Trooper Potter A. | | 7th Hussars |
| Capt. | Morant M. | 7th D.L.I. | Pte | Powney J. | N.F. |
| Gnr | Morgan E. | R.G.A. | " | Pratt J. | 16th D.L.I. |
| Pte | Morgan J. | 8th D.L.I. | " | Pratt T. | 7th Yorks |
| " | Morley W.A. | 10th Essex | Bandsman Preece G. | | 22nd D.L.I. |
| Cpl | Morris C. | 18th D.L.I. | Pte | Preece G.W. | " " |
| Pte | Moug S. | | " | Procter E. | 21st N.F. |
| " | Murdock R. | | " | Procter J. | M.G.C. |
| " | Myers W.H. | 2nd Border Rgt | " | Purvis J. | Winnipeg Rifles |
| " | McClurg W.J. | N.F. | " | Potts A. | Hussars |
| Pte | Naylor W. | Yorks | | | |
| " | Nelson S. | 6th W. Yorks | Pte | Quinn J. | |
| Sgt | Noble A.G., M.M. 8th E. Yorks | | " | Raine J. | M.G.C. |
| | | | " | Sutch J. | 20th N.F. |

| | | | | | | | | | | |
|---|---|---|---|---|---|---|---|---|---|---|
| Pte | Ramsay J.H. | 18th Hussars | 2nd Lt | Shepherd S. | 3rd D.L.I. | Cpl | Tait E. | 22nd D.L.I. | 2nd Lt | Walter T.J. | 5th N.F. |
| " | Ramshaw | | Pte | Shepherd J.H. | W. Yorks | Pte | Tait J.J. | 10th D.L.I. | Pte | Walton A. | 5th D.L.I. |
| " | Reay J. | D.L.I. | Gnr | Short A.E. | R.F.A. | " | Tait P. | K.O.Y.L.I. | 2nd Lt | Walton H.F. | N.F. |
| " | Redshaw T. | 1st Essex Rgt | Pte | Smith A. | 7th Scottish Rifles | " | Taylor W. | 1st E. Yorks | Cpl | Walton J. | 1st W. Yorks |
| " | Reed G.A. | 10th D.L.I. | Sgt | Smith J. | 10th D.L.I. | Sgr Telford T. | | R.E. | Pte | Walton N. | 5th D.L.I. |
| " | Richardson A. | 5th W. Yorks | L Cpl | Smith J.A. | 8th D.L.I. | Pte | Thew J. | 11th D.L.I. | " | Walton N. | 6th W. Yorks |
| Gnr | Ritchie J. | A.I.F. | Pte | Smith J.H. | 6th E. Kent | Sgt Thomas A. | | R.E. | " | Walton T. | |
| Major Roberts F.J. | 1st Qn of R & Surrey | " | Smith W. | 8th D.L.I. | Pte | Thompson W. | 8th D.L.I. | " | Wandless H. | 8th D.L.I. |
| Lt Col Roberts G.C. | Gloucester Rgt | " | Smurthwaite J.G | 2nd Yorks & Lancs | " | Thwaites A. | 8th D.L.I. | " | Warrant E. | |
| Sgt | Robey T. | | " | Snowden A. | 19th D.L.I. | Lieut Tilbrook F.C. | 7th D.L.I. | " | Watson H. | 9th D.L.I. |
| Saddler Robinson A.V. | R.F.A. | " | Spence A. | 2nd Grenadier Gds | Gnr | Todd R. | R.G.A. | " | Watson W.A. | 15th D.L.I. |
| Pte | Robinson T. | Somerset L.I. | " | Spence C.H. | 20th D.L.I. | 2nd Lt | Tombs J.S.W. | R.F.A. | Sgt Maj Watts E.W. | 10th N.F. |
| Sapper Robson J.A. | R.E. | " | Stephenson C. | Lincs Rgt | Pte | Trevitt S. | 18th D.L.I. | Pte | Weelands A. | 15th D.L.I. |
| Trooper Rollin J. | 9th Lancers | " | Stephenson C.W. | 16th D.L.I. | Cpl | Trow Rich | 1st E. Yorks | " | Welsh F.E. | 10th D.L.I. |
| Sgt | Rowan J.L. | | " | Stephenson R. Snr | 5th N.F. | Gnr | Trow Robt | R.G.A. | Sgt | Welsh H.H. | 15th D.L.I. |
| Pte | Rountree F. | R.A.M.C. | " | Stephenson R. Jnr | 2nd N.F. | 2nd Lt | Tumilty A. | Dublin Fusrs | Pte | Welsh J. | 7th Yorks |
| " | Rountree W. | R.F.A. | Bombr Stewart J. | | R.F.A. | | | | " | Williamson F. | R.A.S.C. |
| " | Rule C. | | L Cpl | Stewart J.B. | 6th Yorks | Sapper Vasey C. | | R.E. | " | Wills F.E. | 10th D.L.I. |
| " | Russell J.W. | 5th D.L.I. | 2nd Lt | Stobart J.G. | Rifle Brigade | Pte | Vasey J. | D.L.I. | Sgt | Wills H.H. | 8th D.L.I. |
| 2nd Lt | Reed H.D.T. | 2nd Won. Rgt | Cpl | Strong G. | 9th Yorks | " | Vasey R. | 7th E. Yorks | " | Wilson J. | W. Yorks |
| Pte | Salisbury J.R. | N.F. | Pte | Strong J. | 10th D.L.I. | Sgt | Vasey T.H. | 12th D.L.I. | Pte | Wilson T.C. | D.L.I. |
| " | Saxby C. | 24th N.F. | 2nd Lt | Stuart K.B. | 6th D.L.I. | Pte | Vest A. | 1st E. Yorks | " | Wise J. | 18th D.L.I. |
| " | Scarth J. | 2nd Cold. Gds | Pte | Summerbell T. | 6th N.F. | " | Vest C. | 2nd D.L.I. | " | Woodward T. | 18th D.L.I. |
| " | Scott D. | | 2nd Lt | Summerscales F.D. | 22nd D.L.I. | | | | " | Wright A.J. | N.F. |
| " | Sewell J. | | Signaller Sutton F. | | R.N. | Pte | Wade J. | 3rd D.L.I. | Sgt | Wright W.G. | N.F. |
| " | Sewell J.B. | 8th D.L.I. | Pte | Sweeting C.R. | 1st D.L.I. | " | Waggott J.H. | 2nd D.L.I. | | | |
| " | Shankie J. | 2nd D.L.I. | " | Shotton G. | 15th D.L.I. | " | Walburn J.H. | 2nd N.F. | Pte | Young R. | 5th D.L.I. |
| " | Shaw F.A. | 12th D.L.I. | Driver Tait A. | | R.F.A. | L Cpl Walker F., M.M. | 10th Hussars | Sgt | Yule R. | 19th D.L.I. |
| " | Robinson J.H. | H.L.I. | | | | Lieut Wilson R.A. | 4th D.L.I. | | | |

*(Photographs by Laurie Rampling)*

Four of the men were recognized for their bravery by being awarded the Military Medal. Alexander Gordon **Noble**, was born in 1889 in Gosforth in Northumberland. He was the eldest of seven children born to Alexander and Hannah Noble, and they lived at 7

Lawson Terrace, Durham. Initially he served as a private (20360) with the Durham Light Infantry, before transferring to the East Yorkshire Regiment. He was later promoted to the rank of acting sergeant (16687) with their 8th Battalion, first arriving in France on 9 September 1915. He was twenty-seven years of age when he was killed in action on 14 July 1916. His body was never recovered, he has no known grave and his name is commemorated on the Thiepval Memorial. J. **Oliver** was a lance bombardier (765597) with 'B' Battery, 250th Brigade. Royal Field Artillery. He was killed in action on 10 June 1918, when just twenty-two years of age. He is buried at the Niederzwheren Cemetery, Kassel, in Germany. British soldiers were re-buried here after the war, having initially having been buried at one of seventeen other cemeteries in and around Germany, where they were originally buried. His parents, Thomas and Mary Oliver, lived at 13 Mavin Street, Durham. F. **Walker**, a lance corporal with the 10th Hussars. Although this is the information which is recorded on the City of Durham Roll of Honour, I could find no direct match. The nearest I discovered was a private (16524) F. Walker who served with the 1st/7th Battalion, Duke of Wellingtons (West Riding Regiment). He was killed in action on 29 April 1918 and is buried at La Clytte Military Cemetery, in the West-Vlaanderen region of Belgium. Walter Moffat **Carrick** was a sergeant (18/464) with the 18th Battalion, Durham Light Infantry. He was killed in action on 28 June 1917. His sister, Miss E.J. Carrick, lived at 28 The Avenue, Durham. Walter is buried at the Bailleul Road, East Cemetery, St Laurent Blangy, in the Pas de Calais region of France.

\* \* \*

Marmaduke and Isabella Featherstonhaugh, lived with their six children at 12 Grays Terrace, Durham. They had four sons, Albany, who was the eldest and who worked for the Post Office, next came Marmaduke, who was six years younger, then there was William, who was six years younger still and the youngest son, John, who was born in 1903.

Marmaduke Featherstonhaugh, who was born in 1890, was six years older than his brother William. He was a private (8/2237) in the 1st/8th Battalion, Durham Light Infantry. He was killed in action on 1

September 1915, and is buried in the Cite Bonjean Military Cemetery at Armentières, in the Nord Region of France.

Part of the War Diary for the 1st/8th Battalion, Durham Light Infantry for Wednesday, 1 September 1915, records the following information.

> Armentières Wednesday 1 September 1915
> Still in trench 67 etc. Weather very damp and somewhat cold. The last 24 hours have been very quiet, all the operations being entirely on our side. Our snipers and rifle batteries were busy. No.2237 Pte. Featherstonhaugh was very badly wounded in the head.'

This entry in itself was very unusual, because very rarely do war diary ever contain the names of Private soldiers. It was normal procedure that if an officer was killed or wounded that he would be named, but usually when a private, corporal, sergeant or any other man who was part of what was referred to as the 'other ranks,' was killed or wounded, they were referred to merely as such.

The same entry did not record the fact that Marmaduke had died the same day. I checked the war diary for the following two days to see if his death had been recorded subsequently, but it hadn't.

William Samuel Featherstonhaugh was a private (4094) who served in the 1st/8th Battalion, Durham Light Infantry, when he was killed on 29 September 1916. He has no known grave and he is commemorated on the Thiepval Memorial.

*An unknown soldier of the Durham Light Infantry.*

The War Diary entry for the 1st/8th Battalion for Friday 29 September 1916, records the following very brief entry. 'In Trenches (SPENCE TRENCH, 26Th AVENUE & CRESCENT ALLEY). In the evening the 13th made a bombing attack on the FLERS LINE. (Full details will be given in October War Diary.)' The entry for the following day did record the fact that the battalion's total casualties for the two-week period 16–30 September, were officers killed three, wounded eight, whilst for the other ranks, killed 44, wounded 137 and wounded and missing a further 41. This was an even more interesting entry as there was no mention of even the ranks of the officers who had been killed.

Here is part of a report that was written by Captain G.D. Gould about the bombing raid which took place on 29 September 1916, the one in which William was undoubtedly killed, even though he is not named specifically.

> At 6pm 29th Sept 1916 Second Lieutenant W. G. Russell with 25 men, bombed up 26th Avenue towards point twenty. He successfully entered the German trench and bombed right and left. The balance of 'A' Company followed. They succeeded on the left flank as far as point M.22.a.c.2, and thence up LITTLE C.T. The right flank progressed as far as M22.a.3 ½.1, and thence up the CT. Everything was going well, and the two platoons of 'D' Company, ('C' and 'B' Company's following close behind), came up to further re-enforce the new position. The Bosche was holding the place strongly and registered hard. Suddenly the counter-attack developed and Germans appeared all around the position running and bombing across the open. The two outer flanks withdrew but maintained their position in the German trench.

The report continued with its fine detail. At the end it gave the reasons for the failure of the attack, the first three points of which were as follows;

(1) Under-estimated the strength of the enemy.
(2) Shortage of bombs and lack of supply of same.
(3) Insufficiency of Artillery support and cover fire of Stokes guns [i.e. trench mortars].

The casualties sustained during the attack were recorded as two officers killed, one of whom was believed to have died of his wounds, whilst four other officers were wounded out of a total of thirteen. None of these officers were named. When it came to the men it simply said 'other ranks killed, wounded, and missing about 50%'.

To not even record the men's names could be classed as being slightly disrespectful to their memories, but for it apparently not even be an important-enough matter, to warrant recording the correct numbers in each category, truly beggars belief when judged by today's standards.

# Index

Adamson, Charles Young, 104
Ahlers, Nicholas Emil H.A., 25, 26
Alexander, Captain H., 43
Apperley, Captain N.W., 86
Ardee, Lord, 42
Atkinson, Jane, 61

Bantam Battalions, 59
Barclay, Captain Cyril Lancelot
    Thorald, 102
Bellaby, Corporal, 22
Boruwlaski, Josef, 87
Boyd, Lieutenant William, 99
Brass, Lieutenant James Robson, 52
Brown, Sir Frank, 98
Brown, Lieutenant Philip Anthony, 54
Bruce, Peter, 27
Buckle, Rifleman Percy, 42
Burrell, Captain J.H., 100

Cadle, Coroner Mr, 12
Cadle, Ernest Geoffrey, 47
Caldcleugh, The Mayor Councillor
    Charles, 11, 23
Callinan, Thomas William, 51
Calvert, Sarah, 27, 28
Cambridge University, 51
Canteen Inn, the, 61
Charlton, Alderman Ralph, 84
Charlton, Mr William Bromwell, 24
Chisledon Military Hospital, 18
Chrisp, Company Sergeant Major
    Thomas, 77
City of Durham Roll of Honour, 135
Cousins, Corporal F.G., 82

Cranston, Private Andrew, 76

Dean of Durham, the, 11, 70
Delves, Bridgett, 13
Derby Scheme, the, 66
Dingle, Lieutenant Arthur James, 34,
    35, 37, 38
Douthwaite, Private Philip Herbert,
    101
Durham Cathedral, 133
Durham City Licensed Victuallers
    Association, 21
Durham County Council War
    Memorial, the, 130
Durham Light Infantry, the, 69, 76,
    77, 79, 83, 85, 100, 101, 138
Durham, Lord, 28, 30
Durham Pals, the, 60
Durham School, 36, 40, 41, 125
Durham Town Hall, 11

Elliot, Private Robert, 83

Featherstonhaugh, Marmaduke, 138
*Formidable*, HMS, 47, 48

Galbraith, Alderman Samuel, 91
Gallipoli, 34
Gee, Acting Captain Reginald Claude
    Moline, 102
George, David Lloyd, 61
Gibson, Florence, 38
Gibson, Michael, 38
Goodyear, The Mayor Councillor
    F.W., 81

Gradon, The Mayor Councillor J.G., 67, 68, 86

Handley, Private M., 83
Heaviside, Private Michael Wilson, 78, 80
Hobson, Caroline, 27
Hosking, Lieutenant Cyril Gordon, 48
Humphreys, Lieutenant John Theodore Gordon, 101

Johnson, Colonel J. Burgoyne, 69

Kenny, Private Thomas, 53, 54, 55
King's Certificate, the, 46

Lambert, Captain John Mounsey, 45
Lambton, Francis, 28, 30
Lambton, Geoffrey, 28, 29
Lancaster, Annie, 12, 13
Lancaster, George William, 19
Lancaster, James, 18
Lancaster, John, 12, 13, 16, 17
Lancaster, Robert, 12, 13, 17
Lancaster, Thomas, 19

Marshall, Lieutenant William, 52
McMann, Mr Parker, 104
Meadowfield Police Station, 114
Military Service Act, the, 58, 63
Military Tribunals, 67, 72, 85
Mobbs, Edgar, 36
Mons, Battle of, 22, 29

Nightingale, Florence, 109

Ogg, Mr James, 74
Oxland, Lieutenant Nowell, 34, 35

Parrington, Private George Bramwell, 30
Peacocke, Lieutenant Loftus Gwen Leslie, 102

Proctor, Mayor Alderman George Henderson, 120

Richardson, 2nd Lieutenant Basil Hutton, 52
Richardson, Christopher, 61, 62
Russell, 2nd Lieutenant W.G., 140

Savage, Private Richard, 82
Scarth, Charles Henry, 47
Scarth, John William, 44
Shafto, Captain Arthur Duncombe, 39, 40, 42
Shields, Lieutenant Hugh John Sladen, 42
Smith, Sergeant W.H., 83
Soissons Memorial, the, 101
Somme, Battle of the, 58
St. Bedes College, Durham, 21, 73
Steadman, Mr Justice, 26

Taylor, Captain Hugh, 30
Three Tuns Hotel, the, 20

Vane-Tempest-Stewart, Charles Stewart, 49
Vasey, Private John, 85
Verdun, Battle of, 57
Vickers, Professor Kenneth V, 64, 65
Vest, Arthur, 48
Voluntary Aid Detachments, 107

Waite, Mayor Councillor Peter James, 23
Wheat Sheaf Yard, 15
Wilkin, Coronet Assistant Surgeon Henry, 108
Willets, William, 71

Ypres (Menin Gate) Memorial, the, 30, 31